CLAIM YOUR FREE 30 SECOND PRESENTATION MASTER

Simply complete this coupon and send it to us to receive your free guide to perfect presentation. Packed with tips and practical suggestions the 30 SECOND PRESENTATION MASTER helps you make first-class presentations every time.

☐ *I would like to receive further information on the Ready Made Activities Resource Packs*

Name: _____ Position: _____

Company/Organisation: _____

Address (including postcode): _____

_____

Country: _____

Telephone: _____ Fax: _____

Nature of business: _____

Title of book purchased: _____

Comments: _____

_____

------------------------- **Fold Here Then Staple** -------------------------

We would be very grateful if you could answer these questions to help us with market research.

1 Where/How did you hear of this book?
☐ in a bookshop
☐ in a magazine/newspaper
(please state which):

_____

☐ information through the post
☐ recommendation from a colleague
☐ other (please state which):

_____

2 Which newspaper(s)/magazine(s) do you read regularly?:

_____

_____

3 When buying a business book which factors influence you most?
(Please rank in order)
☐ recommendation from a colleague
☐ price
☐ content
☐ recommendation in a bookshop
☐ author
☐ publisher
☐ title
☐ other(s):

_____

4 Is this book a
☐ personal purchase?
☐ company purchase?

5 Would you be prepared to spend a few minutes talking to our customer services staff to help with product development? YES/NO

Claim your 30 Second Presentation Master
FREE from Pitman Publishing

Simply complete the reverse of this coupon and send it to us – no stamp needed – to claim your FREE 30 SECOND PRESENTATION MASTER – packed with tips and practical suggestions to help make a first-class presentation every time.

Ready Made Activities Resource Packs

The really practical way to run YOUR coaching session. Each Resource Pack contains all the information you can find in the paperback Ready Made Activities... books, plus much, much more!

- **Free Video**
  Use it to introduce the session or reinforce your message
- **Overhead Transparencies**
  Studio designed for a professional presentation – no fuss, no poor handwriting, no spelling mistakes!
- **Photocopiable Handouts**
  Summaries of all the main points for your group to take away.
  No need to write notes, accuracy guaranteed.

Plus
- **£100 OFF WHEN YOU PURCHASE A SELECTED VIDEO FROM LONGMAN TRAINING!**

Tick the box overleaf for more information on the Ready Made Activities Resource Packs

---

Free Information Service
Pitman Professional Publishing
FREEPOST
128 Long Acre
LONDON
WC2E 9BR, UK

No stamp
necessary
in the UK

Ready made activities for
SELLING SKILLS

Ready made activities for SELLING SKILLS

Patrick Forsyth

the Institute of Management

FOUNDATION

PITMAN PUBLISHING

PITMAN PUBLISHING
128 Long Acre, London WC2E 9AN

A Division of Longman Group Limited

First published in Great Britain 1994

British Library Cataloguing in Publication Data
A CIP catalogue record for this book can be obtained from the British Library.

ISBN 0 273 60592 5

10 9 8 7 6 5 4 3 2 1

Typeset by PanTek Arts, Maidstone, Kent.
Printed and bound in England by Clays Ltd, St Ives plc.

It is the Publishers' policy to use paper manufactured from sustainable forests

Buyers Are a Tough Lot

It is any buyer's job to get the best possible deal for his company. That is what they are paid for, they are not actually on the salesmen's side, and will attempt to get the better of them in every way, especially on discounts.

This is well illustrated by the apocryphal story of the fairground strongman. During his act he took an orange, put it in the crook of his arm and bending his arm squeezed the juice out. He then challenged the audience offering £10 to anyone able to squeeze out another drop.

After many had tried unsuccessfully, one apparently unlikely candidate came forward, he squeezed and squeezed and finally out came a couple more drops. The strongman was amazed, and, seeking to explain how this was possible, asked as he paid out the £10 what the man did for a living. 'I am a buyer with Ford Motor Company' he replied.

Buyers are not really like this; they are worse.

From *Everything You need to Know about Marketing*
by Patrick Forsyth (Kogan Page)

Contents

Foreword

I f there is one thing most managers have in common, it is pressure on their time. In an increasingly hectic and competitive world, where change is the order of the day, there is rarely time for everything that needs to be done and setting the right priorities is a prerequisite of success. Training can all too often take a back seat. It is acknowledged as an archetypal 'good thing', yet too often ends up neglected. So anything that makes it easier to implement and thus more certain to occur is all to the good.

This volume, in a series under the title *Ready Made Activities*, is designed to do exactly that, providing a practical approach to developing the essential sales skills which are so crucial to commercial success in a competitive environment.

It is designed to set out guidelines to conducting a complete sales skills training session, and it is presented in the form of a training plan that is:

- **prescribed**, that is the core content can be followed stage by stage, saving time in preparation, and ensuring that the coverage necessary to present the techniques and approaches fundamental to sales success is presented thoroughly

- **participative**, including clear information about how involvement can be included in a way that will improve the learning that the session will prompt

- **flexible**, arranged so that it can easily accommodate additional elements, particularly those designed to produce a focus on the individual product or service with which participants are involved and any other specifics of the organisation, industry or customers which makes every situation unique

- **practical**, including all the information necessary to conduct the session – with suggestions regarding examples, visuals and the training techniques that are necessary to make it successful all in a style which provides an appropriate and useful basis for both line managers and those with little or no training or presentational experience to work from, as well as an aid to training specialists, perhaps especially those without a training background.

After the introduction a clear **how to use this material** section sets out the way in which material is presented and how it can be used. Thereafter the material follows the sequence of the training session it describes, with support material following for those who need additional guidance on the presentation of the material.

Having been involved in marketing, sales and communication skills training in a variety of forms for some 20 years I am pleased to be involved in this new series. Pitman has developed an enviable reputation for the quality of material in recent years, and having contributed to their Financial Times series (*Marketing Professional Services*) and their Institute of Management series (*Marketing for Non-marketing Managers*) I was pleased to work with them again. Selling is a vital component of an organisation's marketing strategy, and must play its part strongly and effectively if the results achieved by the totality of that effort are to meet the objectives set. If this material contributes to that process for those using it then it will serve a useful purpose.

Patrick Forsyth
Touchstone Training & Consultancy
17 Clocktower Mews
London
N1 7BB

Acknowledgements

I never set out to be a trainer. My route to it was through marketing. The marketing of training products, seminars, conferences and publications put me in touch with the world of consultancy, and having joined a consulting firm in a marketing position I was then encouraged to become involved in client work. Much of my time as a consultant was spent with the Marketing Improvements Group Plc. During that time I wrote a number of books, drawing in part on company material. Some text and diagrams from that material is included – reproduced or adapted – in this book, and I would like to acknowledge that company's permission to do this here.

So, any ability I may have now to set out this sort of material is the result of my involvement in work with a variety of clients over what is now some 20 years in consultancy and training. The experience I have gained from this, and the suggestions and guidance I have received – and continue to receive – from consultancy colleagues and associates along the way is simply invaluable. So often it is the people whose time is most valuable who are most generous with it in assisting others. Thanks to them all therefore; and to the participants on the many sales courses I have run over the years, and from whose participation and comments I also always learn so much. Writing, a more recent part of my portfolio of activities, necessitates pulling together and presenting from this experience what might be most accurately described as 'best current practice'. What is presented here is not, I am sure, the only way of viewing the sales process; but it is one that is field tested through the many courses and seminars I have conducted for sales people in the past. I hope by writing about selling in this way I will not cease to number sales courses amongst those I conduct for organisations in a variety of industries and countries each year, though I certainly hope it will enable a number of people to do their own thing and get as much satisfaction from it as I have so often had from training.

Finally, this title is one of a series. In parallel with my writing this material Sheila Cane, a consultant with whom I work occasionally on an associate basis,was writing the companion volume on negotiation. To ensure the appropriate degree of relationship between the content and style of the two titles, we liaised regularly and her comments proved a valuable source of assistance as my work progressed. So thanks are due for her many constructive comments and for all those cups of tea.

P.F.

1

INTRODUCTION

f bringing in the business was easy, we would all be rich, and this publication would be of little value. It is, however, the very reverse of easy. Markets of all sorts are increasingly competitive, customers are increasingly fickle and the old saying about even producing a better mousetrap not ensuring that the world will beat a path to your door has never been more true. So, marketing – simplistically defined as the process which sets out to bring in the business (having first had something to say about the product or service to be sold) – is the order of the day. Few, if any, companies leave the business generation process to chance; a whole panoply of techniques are routinely used to increase the chances of success. And even that may not be sufficient. Promotional techniques need to be creatively applied and their effectiveness will also be dependent on how appropriately they are targeted at those, who in turn must be well identified, who are genuine prospects for whatever is being supplied.

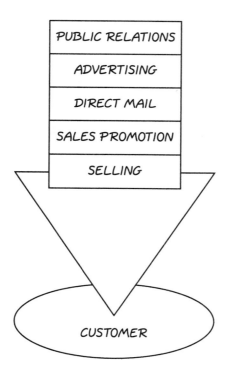

Figure I.1 The mix of persuasive communications

The mix of promotional techniques includes methods which are different from each other in the way they work. Figure I.1 shows the main techniques and illustrates how they operate in separate ways in terms of their relationship to the customer. Some, such as much public relations activity, acting as much as anything to create a background image that acts as a foundation for other techniques to build on. Others only work by focusing more closely on the customer. All are important. In some industries, and at some times, one may be more important than another, but rarely is there any one 'magic formula' that brings in the business; a mix is more usually necessary. But one technique is, if not more important, then different in nature and forms the final link between suppliers and customers. That is selling.

This is the only personal, two way, and often one to one, communication in the mix. For many organisations the other promotional tactics create the awareness and interest, but only selling can convert that view into the buying actions that bring in the revenue and thus profit. There is more to selling than may sometimes meet the eye. Its role and objectives are broad. It creates orders, or should do, but it may also need to be instrumental in creating relationships, building loyalty and maintaining and developing business in the longer term.

There is another factor, too, that is important. Selling, like other promotional activity, must not only spark interest, it must differentiate, and differentiate powerfully, between a particular supplier and competition. Many, perhaps most, products and services have taken on the characteristics of commodities. It is often difficult for potential customers to differentiate between competing cars, computers, caterers or copiers; or at least to do so on any truly objective basis. Technical specifications, and often price, are increasingly similar. Differences will certainly exist, not least in image, service and amongst the people in the competing organisations. Selling must, as part of its role, highlight such differences and provide solid grounds on which customers can base their choice of one supplier rather than another.

This is, however, to understate the case. Selling, and the salespeople who undertake the task, *must themselves be part of that difference*. They must, by the way they go about their work, contribute to the likelihood of their customers wanting to do business with them rather than someone else. Their role is therefore not just important, it is crucial. All the influences deployed to persuade potential customers to do business operate cumulatively. They progressively build up the level of awareness, interest, understanding and trust that must reach a particular level before customers feel they have weighed up the situation and buying action is then taken. In a competitive world every element that contributes in this way may be significant and the line between a customer being persuaded, or not, may be a fine one. Many throughout the organisation play their part in bringing in the business, but the salespeople are in a prime position to ensure that their individual input is significant and, as a result, creates a volume of business that will see the organisation survive and prosper.

It has been said that nothing happens until someone sells something, and commercially at least this may well be true. But selling does not achieve its aims by magic any more than does any other marketing technique. There is rarely any such thing as the so-called 'born salesman', and going through the motions is never going to bring the right returns however good the product or service involved. Selling must utilise the available techniques and approaches effectively if it is to maximise its success, and this does not just happen. Further, selling in the markets of the 1990s is a fragile process.

As was said earlier, the line between the customer agreeing to buy or not may well be very fine. Similarly things the salesperson does which influence whether the customer ends up on one side of the line rather than the other, may be small, indeed may seem insignificant. One word used rather than another. One segment of the sales presentation that is less than clear, that prompts too many questions or seems just that small amount less credible and the effect of what is being done is diluted just enough to weaken the case irretrievably. Of course, the positive side of this is true also. One small difference, one added gesture can work to swing the sale and prompt an order. All this puts a considerable onus on the salesperson to make what he does very precise, yet at the same time it must remain a fluid, fluent two-way conversation that gives the customer what he wants.

Increasing the chances of success

Selling must be undertaken in just the right way and its techniques deployed literally customer by customer, meeting by meeting, day by day. It has been said already that this is not an area of magic formulae, but one factor has almost that kind of power. Training makes the difference. If there is one factor that does mark out the more successful salespeople from their less successful peers, it is an understanding of what makes them success-ful. This allows them to deploy techniques consciously, but always appropriately, to ensure they have the desired effect. Experience will clearly help cultivate this ability, but it is not guaranteed to do so. Training can accelerate experience, and effective training can certainly contribute to ensuring the ability to operate in a way that suits the market and brings in good results. But training does not just happen any more than orders do. Hence this manual, the intention of which is to ensure that training in this area is made just a little easier and thus more likely to take place.

It takes a practical view, in part behavioural, but also technique driven. Above all it is intended to help salespeople go about their job with a heightened awareness that will allow them to deploy the right techniques throughout their meetings. It is also intended to help them focus on things from the customers' point of view, because only an approach which respects the customer, and which avoids being patronising or pushy, will end with the customer wanting to do business with the salesperson con-cerned and seeing the salesperson as professional. The best, and perhaps the simplest definition of selling I know is that it is 'helping people to buy'.

Its apparent simplicity belies the way it summarises so much of what makes selling successful. This manual is concerned to help you help your salespeople to practice such an approach, and to set out clear guidelines to allow you to take them through the core skills and give them a foundation from which to work in future.

The next two sections set out who the material is designed to be used by and the session run for, and how exactly to use the training plan set out in the next chapter.

WHO CAN BEST USE THIS MATERIAL

It is difficult to make any material such as this all things to all people. Sales techniques *does* need to be applied differently depending on what is being sold to whom. So here the material does have a particular focus, and the format is designed to allow the resulting training session to be still more accurately directed towards your own business.

The emphasis is on the selling of products and services 'business-to-business', rather than the sale of FMCG (Fast Moving Consumer Goods) through retail channels. The examples chosen as illustrations are simple and easy to relate to, and the material allows a strong link to be made between the general principles and the specific situation within an individual organisation, and the detail of the actual product or service being sold.

The topic

The content relates to the so-called face-to-face selling stage of the overall sales process, dealing with key techniques for the sales meeting itself. It does not cover such ancillary areas as planning and executing territory management and coverage, prospecting and making appointments, or negotiation (though there is a companion volume in this same series on negotiation and another on account management and development).

The ideal participants

The content is designed to act as source material for a session directed at salesmen. This is becoming an unacceptable word in some circles, so I will elaborate. Salesperson may be politically correct, but it describes a category that is too wide for present purposes, including for instance retail staff. Sales representative is old-fashioned, both as a word and in concept; there is much more to the job in the nineties than it implies. Perhaps we may settle for 'field salesperson', as what it lacks in elegance it makes up for in descriptiveness. If your sales team work externally, calling on buyers (whoever that may be in your business) whether once or in a way that leads, or is designed so to do, to a continuing business relationship, then this material will enable you to conduct a training session suitable for them.

It is, in fact, the job and its attendant tasks that matter. It may carry the title of Salesman, Sales Engineer, Sales Consultant, Account (or Territory) Manager or many others. It may be that the salespeople are also the 'production' resource, as in the kind of business where, say, designers or consultants have to both bring in the business and do the resulting work. Providing their job, or a major part of it, is selling, the basis of the session will be right. With minimal adjustment it can be directed to new field sales staff, those not so new but with no, or little, formal training, or those with more experience as a refresher.

The ideal 'leader'

The nature of the material makes it suitable for two broad groups of people:

- **managers** in some sort of line or staff role which makes it logical for them to take responsibility for, and undertake, this sort of training. This may mean the Sales Manager, Area Manager with relation to their local team or some other middle manger; or it might be a director or general management person in a smaller company, or even a senior sales team member asked to take on this role.

For these the material offers complete guidance, and flexibility if required. It will save preparation time and make the conduct of a successful session more certain. It offers guidance on the how of running (e.g. presentation techniques) as well as structure and coverage.

- **trainers**, who can either simply use it as a time saver (or to cross check thinking with another source) for the more experienced, or to fill in gaps for those less experienced or without links with the sales function.

Whichever category you fall into, and experience shows that in many companies it is non-trainers who are increasingly becoming involved in this kind of exercise, the material is designed to be of practical help in improving sales effectiveness and thus sales results.

HOW TO USE THIS MATERIAL

This material is designed to be self-explanatory and to minimise preparation time. Clearly the user will need to read the material in its entirety before embarking on conducting a training session, and you may also want to make additional notes to have with you as you run the session. However, the material follows the sequence of the session it describes and is arranged so that its various elements stand out as signposts to the effective conduct of the session. Even the typeface is chosen so that everything is presented in a size that may be comfortably read while standing in front of a group session.

As an overall approach it is suggested that you:

- complete reading this section first
- read through the total training plan
- check whether how you will conduct the session will be aided by referring to the later material providing information about training techniques, and referring to any elements you feel will be useful
- decide which elements of the programme you will use
- add any necessary notes you will need to have in front of you
- relate what you want to do to the nature of the group and the numbers which will attend, so that for instance participative elements will fit in
- check and arrange the equipment and environmental factors (a checklist to assist this process completes this section),

then you will be in a position to make final arrangements and conduct the session.

THE ELEMENTS OF THE MATERIAL

As you read on you will notice that the material includes the following elements which are commented on in turn.

Main content

The main thread of the material in terms of suggested running instructions for the leader, and detail of the coverage to be presented, appears sequentially. All main headings are **in large bold type** to facilitate rapid, easy reference as you conduct the session. All key instructional words:

- **introduce**
- **discuss**
- **emphasise**
- **stress**
- **explain**
- **ask**
- **make a note**
- **summarise**

appear in **bold type** to make sure they stand out. Further bold type is used within the text **to provide additional emphasis** and guide the eye to the key parts of the text. In addition to this text clearly indicated **BACK-GROUND NOTES** appear in boxed pages to give you more detail of the topic under review. This information intentionally goes a little beyond the content indicated in the running guidelines, both to provide background and allow you to base what you finally present on whatever is most appropriate for the group. This aspect of the content is addressed to those doing the selling, i.e. as you will need to put it over. Once you have read and digested this additional information you may well wish to use it more as general background information rather than follow it slavishly, using the remaining, main text as the core skeleton that will enable you to direct the session.

Note: the **Background Notes** are, in part, drawn and adapted from the author's book *The Selling Edge* (a Piatkus paperback). Thus, if the content and style of this is suitable for those who make up your training group, this book might make a suitable handout. Perhaps this might be most usefully issued after the workshop as a reminder, something that will focus participants' minds on the issues raised for a longer period of time.

Examples

There is a need in any training to exemplify points made both to explain, maintain interest and make lessons relate to the actual job to be done by the participant. Examples appear progressively through the text – as do spaces where you may wish to add examples relating to your own organisation and especially to the product or service which you supply. This provides a key opportunity to tailor the material more specifically to your own circumstances.

Symbols

Additional elements within the text are all flagged by appropriate symbols in the margin, again so that you can focus on all the different elements easily and quickly as you go through the total material. These include the following:

Visuals

Certain points are worth showing as well as saying (repetition and seeing as well as hearing are proven aids to learning). Suggestions as to which points are dealt with in this way appear throughout the text. The simplest way of implementing these is to write up material on a flipchart, or table-top presenter. This can be done as the session progresses or made ready in advance and simply turned through as you go.

Of course, if other methods are available, for instance an overhead projector, such material can be prepared as slides or written as you proceed using an acetate roll or sheets (see page 157).

Two forms of suggestion are made:

- a general suggestion made within the text to write something
- specific suggestions shown in the form that might result on a flip chart.

You can, of course, list more than is suggested and should look particularly for more visual images (within your artistic ability if you are using the flip chart or preprepared material).

Participation

Certain topics lend themselves to discussion or involvement, indeed any meeting such as is discussed here needs to include participation to maintain interest, improve learning and the link between the material covered and implementation. Clear suggestions appear at appropriate points setting out participative elements that can be included - whether they are the simple asking of a question, brief discussion or something more involved such as an exercise or role-playing.

Note: with an interactive skill such as selling, role-playing is a well proven way of improving awareness and bridging the gap between training and real life and real prospects and customers. It is specifically suggested, towards the end of the training plan, that each participant has an opportunity to undertake a role-play situation. Basic details of how to set this up are given in context and more information about how to make role-play effective appears later (see page 169).

The flexibility of the material

Whatever the configuration of your ideal training session, it may rarely be possible to proceed with exactly this as your structure. Some compromise is nearly always involved, especially regarding time and money. Thus it is not always possible to spend as long on things, or include as much participation, as you might wish. In addition, everyone's priorities vary. What may be important in one organisation may be less so in another, and taking more time over one element or topic may necessitate taking less over another.

The material is designed to be flexible. While it provides a comprehensive skeleton, the format allows additional tailoring towards the needs of a specific group - for instance by adding examples as referred to above. To facilitate this process still further, certain elements of the programme may be regarded as options, that is they may be omitted without disrupting the flow of the main thread of the content. This allows the material to be condensed somewhat, or for more tailoring (more added examples or participation, for example) to take place without extending the overall time the training takes.

Note: at key break points throughout the material there is space for you to note timings. The precise timings will be conditioned by:

- the number attending
- the exact programme conducted
- the amount of planned, and reactive, participation
- the role-play element

and, to some extent, by the experience of the presenter.

Given manageable numbers, certainly 8–12, it should be possible to go through the suggested main content in one day, with the role play adding on a pro rata basis. If necessary or desirable you may want to schedule a longer, or shorter, session and could split the coverage in other ways (for example, a series of evening sessions).

Make the material your own

Now, with this organisation in mind you can proceed to the main training plan. Remember it is *your* session we are talking about, so one final point: as has been made clear, this book is designed to be a working tool. It is unlikely to do as good a job as is possible unless you overcome the natural reluctance which most people have to write in a book. It is designed for it; no one will mind. So do add your own notes and examples where appropriate and consider highlighting – in a second colour or with a fluorescent highlighting pen – to indicate the emphasis you want and make key points stand out. If you use it to provide not simply guidance to conducting the session, but guidance to conducting *your* session, it will be that much more useful and your participants will find what you put over that much more helpful to their work in the field.

Note: If you aim to, or might, conduct workshops from this material more than once, then some additional note taking may well be useful. This need results from the participative nature of any training. For example, if you make a point, then quote an example and then ask for thoughts about additional examples, you may well find that some good examples are volunteered. If so, some or all of these may be worth recording to use as part of the next presentation. In other words your annotated material will become more valuable with use.

2

······································

THE TRAINING WORKSHOP

I n this, the main section of this book, the plan for a sales workshop is laid out session by session. If you have read the explanatory sections in Chapter 1 you will recognise the various elements here as they appear, and will find that the guidelines on **how** to proceed through the session alternate with the **content** that needs to be put over.

Once you have been through this section, and personalised it to whatever degree you feel useful (a process that can involve skipping elements as well as adding), then you should be able to conduct the session with these pages, and any visuals you decide to prepare, in front of you acting as your 'lecture/running notes'.

Programme objectives:

These are defined as follows:

- to **review** the essential techniques that make business-to-business selling successful

- to **promote** a proven, flexible and professional approach the makes practical sense in the real world

- to **develop** an understanding of how this approach can be used responsively in relationship with customer needs

- to **prompt** a considered deployment of selling techniques as appropriate to each individual sales situation dealt with.

Programme structure

Before going into the detail of the session it may be useful to get the overall 'shape' of it in mind. The flow chart that follows sets out the various stages and elements graphically and is designed to help keep the entirety of the session in mind throughout the process, so that individual elements are clearly in context.

This 'course map' is arranged so that you can add any notes and details you wish, and elements of the resulting chart might form a useful basis for a visual for use as the group's session progresses.

COURSE MAP

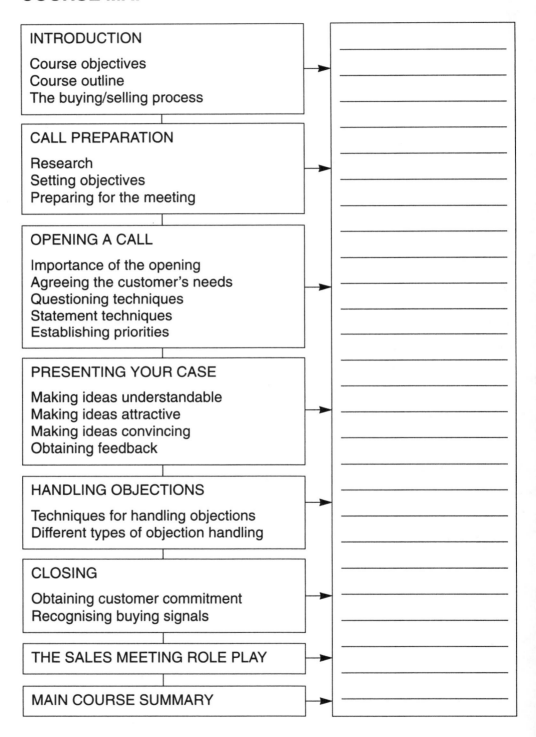

INTRODUCTION

Course objectives
Course outline
The buying/selling process

CALL PREPARATION

Research
Setting objectives
Preparing for the meeting

OPENING A CALL

Importance of the opening
Agreeing the customer's needs
Questioning techniques
Statement techniques
Establishing priorities

PRESENTING YOUR CASE

Making ideas understandable
Making ideas attractive
Making ideas convincing
Obtaining feedback

HANDLING OBJECTIONS

Techniques for handling objections
Different types of objection handling

CLOSING

Obtaining customer commitment
Recognising buying signals

THE SALES MEETING ROLE PLAY

MAIN COURSE SUMMARY

Session 1
· ·
Overall introduction

Introduce yourself and let course participants introduce themselves if they do not already know each other.

Before making clear the course objectives:

Explain any topical factors – internal or external – which make the course important now, for example:

● New machinery increases capacity/need for sales.

● Growth targets demand tapping new markets (perhaps needing new approaches).

● Economic/legal or market changes are likely to increase/decrease or change demand patterns.

● Customer expectations have changed.

● Product change.

Make a note of any actual topical factors you will want to mention:

_____

_____

_____

_____

Explain the course objectives (these are set out at the start of this chapter).

You may want to list these on the flip chart (or even leave them visibly at the front throughout the session).

Emphasise the practical nature of the programme.

Explain the course coverage and link it to the timetable (and any necessary administrative details - breaks, meals, loos etc).

COURSE OUTLINE

- Introduction
- Call preparation
- Opening your call
- Presenting your case
- Handling objectives
- Closing
- Role play
- Summary

Emphasise that the key stages of selling lead up to the most crucial stage of all, 'closing the sale', and that obtaining the appropriate commitment is the ultimate objective at every stage.

Make a note of any other elements you wish to introduce at this introductory stage (e.g. a link to a new or changed product/service):

_____

_____

_____

 Ask for any questions from the group before proceeding.

To make a start to the involvement that the programme will need you may elect to conduct a brief 'ice-breaker' exercise at this point.

E.g. (an exercise)

Ask participants to draw the following:

× × ×

× × ×

× × ×

and join them not using more than four straight lines. Allow a couple of minutes. The solution is:

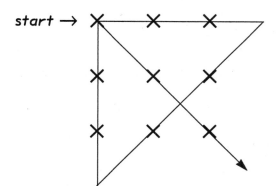

Most see it as a box, and no solution is possible within the square. **Moral**: we must constantly seek solutions outside our immediate experience – the background emphasis of this course.

E.g. (a brief discussion) 'Why do people buy our products/services at all?'

Explain the importance of appreciating the selling process from the customers' point of view. Briefly link to the main stages of the sales process.

Stress that, simply stated, selling is 'helping people to buy'. It is not something we do *to* people. It must be acceptable.

Explain the buying/selling process, column by column from left to right.

Emphasise that the way people make purchase decisions dictates the way selling needs to be approached, rather than selling being applied as something exclusively done to the prospect or customer.

The decision-making process

Decision sequence	Persuasion objectives	Persuasion stages
I am important. Consider my needs.	To create rapport, generate interest or acceptance. To find out about them and their needs.	1 Opening
What are the facts?	To state a case that will be seen as balanced in favour of action.	2 Stating the case
What are the snags?	Preventing or handling negative reactions that may unbalance the argument (objections).	3 Handling objections
What shall I do? I approve.	Obtaining a commitment to action, or to a step in the right direction (purchase)	4 Injunction to act (close)

This chart, which also appears (with more information) in the Background Notes (page 28) encapsulates much of the basis on which the workshop is arranged. It may be worth having a preprepared flipchart or slide – it is rather too much to write up as you proceed – or a handout so that participants see this as an overview.

At the same time explain that it is the job of the salesperson to differentiate the organisation from competition (or to play a part in this process which, of course, is aided by other marketing activity).

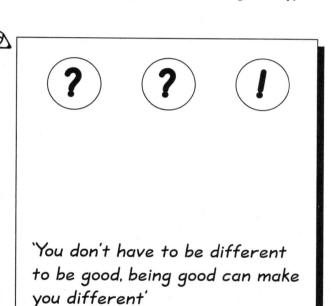

'You don't have to be different to be good, being good can make you different'

This differentiation must be of a noticeable degree and is achieved primarily by the appropriateness of what we do for a particular individual customer.

Making this point will help link to planning, which many salespeople neglect, underestimating its significance. It is this process which ensures we are able to differentiate.

Everyone has to go about selling using their own personality, but manner and approach are important if customers are to be impressed and find the style acceptable.

The diagram (which can be reproduced on the flipchart), sets out how just two factors can help ensure the overall approach is appropriate. First, projection, the whole manner in which salespeople come over (the presence, the expertise, the professionalism, the advice, the 'clout'). Secondly, the empathy (the ability to put yourself is the other person's shoes and see his point of view – and to be seen to do so).

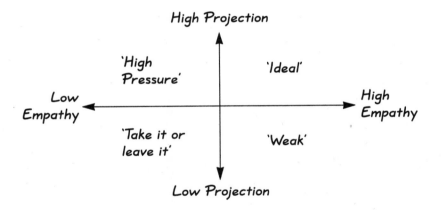

Balancing the two elements gives us four salesman types:

- the archetypal double glazing salesman
- the worst sort of retail selling
- the one liked by the customer, but less than 100 per cent effective
- the ideal.

This concept may provide a useful and interesting additional discussion point.

BACKGROUND NOTES

A basis for the sales process – introduction

A sales meeting is a dynamic thing. It is a meeting involving two people with different thoughts, views and intentions, yet with potentially a common aim; to do business. To make the face-to-face meeting successful is, as we have already seen, dependent on many things, not least on the ability of the salesperson to chart a course through this unpredictable encounter, and to do so in a way that encourages the prospect to feel the process is useful and that he stands to gain from it.

We referred earlier to the structure of the sales and buying process. This must form the foundation of everything that happens face-to-face, and must be kept in mind as an element of the 'route map' you need to guide you through the meeting.

Start by considering how people buy; how they make a decision to purchase, or not. Classically their thinking moves through seven stages.

- I am important and I want to be respected.
- Consider my needs.
- How will your ideas help me?
- What are the facts?
- What are the snags?
- What shall I do?
- I approve (or not).

This seems like common sense; indeed if you think about it, you will find it is what you do. A good analogy is that of 'weighing up' the case or argument, putting all the good points on one side, all the less good on the other and assessing the net effect.

Any attempt that responds unsatisfactorily to any of these stages is unlikely to end in agreement. The buyer's mind has to be satisfied on each point before moving to the next, and to be successful the persuading sequence must match this decision-making sequence, and run parallel to it.

The chart shows the process alongside the persuasive objectives, what you are trying to achieve at each stage and the technique employed in any communication. The two keys to success are the process of matching the other person's progression and describing, selectively, your case, and discussing in a way that relates to the circumstances of the other person.

The decision-making process

Decision sequence	Persuasion objectives	Persuasion stages
I am important. Consider my needs.	To create rapport, generate interest or acceptance. To find out about them and their needs.	1 Opening
What are the facts?	To state a case that will be seen as balanced in favour of action.	2 Stating the case
What are the snags?	Preventing or handling negative reactions that may unbalance the argument (objections).	3 Handling objectives
What shall I do? I approve.	Obtaining a commitment to action, or to a step in the right direction (purchase).	4 Injunction to act (close)

When persuasion works, both parties will have gone through this sequence stage by stage. However, if the attempt to persuade is unsuccessful, it will often be found that:

- The sequence has not taken place at all.
- Some stage has been missed out.
- The sequence has been followed too quickly or too slowly, which means the salesperson is at one stage when the prospect wants to be, and expects the salesperson to be, at another. The two processes must proceed in tandem.

Early on, because people may well need to go through a number of stages – they may want proposals in writing, to confer with a colleague or run a test of the product being sold – you may not always be able to aim immediately for a commitment to buy. You must, however, have some other, clear objective on which to get a commitment. A positive 'yes' to your putting in a written proposal is a good step in the right direction. The persuasion of what you are doing throughout the process must be lined up towards such an end.

Imagine, as a simple example, that a secretary wants the boss to buy a new typewriter. The ultimate objective is for them to say 'Yes, buy it' about a particular machine. But it may be a step in the right direction to get them to review some brochures, check the quality of what the present machine produces, have a demostration, get a quote and so on. Sometimes there are many steps to be gone through before the ultimate objective can be achieved. Progressing through each, like taking steps up a ladder, is significant in reaching the end point, whether it is the top of the ladder or the objective we have set. In selling interim objectives may include agreement to accept a trial, a sample or a demonstration; a request for a quotation or written proposal and so on.

Whatever your objective is, however, it is important to know and to be able to recognise the various stages ahead. With any individual contact you can identify the following.

- What stage has been reached in the decision process?
- What do you need to do if the sequence does not match?
- Has a step been missed?
- Are you going too fast?
- Should you go back in the sequence?
- Can your objectives still be achieved, or were they the wrong objectives?
- How can you help the other person through the rest of the buying process?

Naturally, the whole process is not always covered in only one contact between salesperson and prospect; several meetings or exchanges may be necessary.

KEY POINT

Understand the Structure

- understand how the customer views the process
- use their thinking process to help you sell
- aim everything towards the close
- monitor and adapt as you proceed

The structure of the buying/selling process is the basis for all that follows. On the sales side, an understanding of how people make buying decisions is the foundation of sales success. You should aim firmly towards the close, but always bear the customer's view firmly in mind. This makes what you do at every stage more effective, and helps you to view every sales contact as a unique event.

Be conscious of what you are doing throughout the process.

Making it acceptable

There are two factors that, together, make your manner acceptable. They should be an appropriate blend of 'projection' and of 'empathy'. What exactly do these terms mean? Well, by 'projection' we mean the way we come across to others, and particularly the confidence, credibility and 'clout' with which we come over, or at least appear to come over. By 'empathy' we mean simply the ability to put yourself in the other person's shoes and see things from his point of view. Not only to see him, but also to *be seen to do so*.

It is possible to categorise four distinct types of sales approach on an axis of high and low projection and high and low empathy. This is illustrated in the chart.

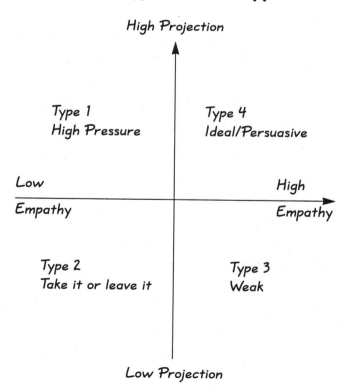

The four types of sales approach

High Projection

Type 1
High Pressure

Type 4
Ideal/Persuasive

Low
Empathy

High
Empathy

Type 2
Take it or leave it

Type 3
Weak

Low Projection

Type 1: the 'high-pressure' salesperson is over-aggressive and insensitive. *He* may feel he wins the argument but, in fact, projection, without empathy, becomes self-defeating and switches people off. The archetypal high-pressure person is the popular image of, say, the double-glazing salesperson.

Type 2: the 'take it or leave it' salesperson has little interest either in the other person, nor, curiousiy, his own ideas. A lack of commitment to the whole process tends to let it run into the sand. The archetypal take it or leave it person is the kind of unhelpful shop assistant with whom most of us are all too familiar.

Type 3: the 'weak' communicator is the sort of person of which it is said, disparagingly, 'they mean well'. And so they do, they have good sensitivity to the other person, and come over as essentially nice, but take the side of the listener so much on occasion that persuasion vanishes and they achieve nothing.

Type 4: what works best is the positive combination of the two factors, with one adding strength to the persuasion deployed while the other maintains the perceived customer orientation that is always necessary.

KEY POINT

Adopt the Right Manner

- be conscious of the manner you adopt
- tailor your approach to the customer
- make sure you appear professional
- always see, and respond, to the customer's views

If we are honest, salespeople are not involved in everyone's favourite profession. At worst the archetypal hard-sell, high-pressure sales approach switches people off. And so it should. Therefore, there is no room for an unprofessional approach. If the manner adopted adds throughout the process to the customer seeing you as the exception rather than the rule, as they might put it, as a professional – then it adds to your effectiveness.

Always use empathy, and project in a way that builds credibility.

Session 2

···

Call preparation

Explain that call preparation involves deciding in advance of a sales meeting what needs to be achieved and the best way of achieving it.

 Stress (and list) the benefits for the salesperson of careful and thorough call planning:

- achieves effective use of limited time so that greater productivity can be achieved
- helps make our ideas more acceptable to the customer
- helps towards achieving call objectives
- helps enhance our professional image

all of which help the salesperson to achieve his ultimate goal – a successful close.

Ask the group for other benefits that they have come across or can think of.

The Planning Process

Point out that a major problem when planning a sales meeting with a potential customer who has not been seen before is lack of information.

> **Explain** that this will always be the case with the proportion of calls salespeople will need to make if they need to expand the customer base to gain a larger share of the market, i.e. there is a possible link here to **prospecting** if appropriate.

Introduce briefly the seven main elements of the call **explaining** that each will be dealt with in detail a little later.

CALL PREPARATION

- Objectives
- Research

  - Opening
  - Presentation
  - Handling Objections
  - Closing

- Support

Explain that the first key step in the planning process is to decide what it is that needs to be achieved at each sales meeting. These objectives are known as **call objectives.**

'SMART' OBJECTIVES

Specific

Measurable

Achievable

Realistic

Timed

Reinforce the points about planning with an **exercise**:

Ask each member of the group to consider a sales situation, a real customer and a future call, and to write down a call objective – appropriate for the envisaged situation – which corresponds to the key objective criteria already mentioned; allow maybe 5–10 minutes for thought, then:

Ask all, or several, participants to describe their chosen situation and objective, check – with the group – whether it is appropriate to the circumstances and meets the criteria. (This can be repeated with more than one example if you wish.)

Emphasise that when planning for sales meetings with potential customers who are not known, it is crucial to devote enough time to research – finding out something about them.

In the first instance this can be desk research prior to the meeting and should cover such details (list on flip chart) as:

  the person to be seen

  customer's company (size, structure, key personnel, financial situation
      etc.)

  industry/product/service (our experience of it)

  purchase influencers

  the competition

  possible needs and future plans

  the sales potential anticipated

  travel arrangements … etc.

Ask the group for any other pre-meeting research areas that should be considered, listing good ideas.

Make a note of any others you may want to draw out:

_____

_____

_____

_____

_____

Explain that research into the customer and his situation should be an on-going process. In particular the sales meeting will need to be a time to ask questions to find out about:

who the decision-makers are

any preferred buying or approvals systems

the customer needs in more detail

preferred call frequency

future plans etc.

Tell the group that you are now going to cover the **advance planning and thinking** that needs to be done **for the key stages of the sales interview** itself:

the opening

the main presentation

handling objections

closing the sale.

Explain that handling each of these stages will be dealt with in detail later in the course.

Write the heading 'OPENING' at the top of the flip chart.

Ask the group to suggest what they will need to be thinking about before the call in relation to the opening stage of the interview with the buyer.

List contributions on the flip chart.

Try to obtain at least the following points from the group:

  put the customer at ease

  get the customer interested and talking

  explore the customer's needs

  establish the customer's priorities

If these points are not easily forthcoming introduce them yourself and then **discuss** them briefly with the group.

These discussion periods should be quite short because these topics will be dealt with in more detail later on in the course.

On another flip chart page **write** 'PRESENTATION'.

Ask as with the 'OPENING' stage try to obtain the following points from the group.

List them on the flip chart.

  Offer the customer desirable results from his point of view

  Prove my case to the customer's satisfaction

  Explain complex points simply

  Show how customer needs will be met

Repeat as above with 'OBJECTIONS'.

  Have I considered what they might be?

  Have I got answers which will satisfy the customer?

  Are they related to the customer's needs?

Repeat as above with 'CLOSE'.

 Get a commitment

Match my objectives

Make it easy for the customer to agree

Leave the customer feeling better than before the call

Repeat as above with 'SUPPORT MATERIAL'

Emphasise that this is an important stage of preparation and planning for us and mention any specific, or new, **items that can be demonstrated**. This may include anything from graphs and charts to samples or photographs.

Make a note of any items the team actually use that you may wish to mention or discuss:

_____

_____

_____

_____

_____

Then:

 Ask the group to consider what pre-call planning needs to be done in terms of the support material that can be used.

 List on the flip chart.

Identify what we need

Identify what the customer may need

Ensure that it is available to take along at the time of the sales meeting

Decide how best to present it

When planning to use support materials, work out beforehand what the benefits are for the customer

Suggest that we should make a point of noticing how support materials have helped customers in the past and then relate this to the needs of new potential customers being visited. Then:

Summarise.

 **Write** the heading 'CALL PLANNING' at the top of the flip chart.

Summarise on the flip chart the key points learned during this section, **asking** the group to contribute.

List them on the flip chart.

 **Ask** for any further questions from the group proceeding.

Conclude by repeating the necessity for planning to take place.

TIME:

BACKGROUND NOTES

The face-to-face sales meeting

Call preparation

Preparation is important. Now, before you turn over or skip this section, let us look at that remark in another way. Call preparation, the final elements of the planning process, can make the difference between getting an order or not. So it is worth a moment of your time. Simply put, it is the expedient of engaging the brain before opening the mouth. It is important enough to give it the status of an 'edge-giver' before we even explore it.

That said, how do we go about it? Planning is traditionally a weak area, and, if your competitors are not good at it, so much the better for you – if you are prepared it will differentiate you, or at least play a part in the process.

The first rule about preparing the call, each and every call, is therefore simple: you must do it. It is a necessary discipline – an attitude of mind, even – that prompts objective thinking about what *can* be achieved, what *must* be achieved and *how to* deploy techniques and resources to maximise the likelihood of success.

As has already been said, successful salespeople, in any field, are usually those who do their homework. This may mean a few moments' thought sitting in the car just before you go in to see a prospect; a few minutes going through the files, perhaps the night before; or a couple of hours sitting round the table with colleagues to thrash out the best approach.

Such preparation allows you to ensure that the meeting wlll focus on the individual and that you are fluent and confident in what you do. It will also save time (a valuable resource for both parties), compared with a less well-prepared and well-structured meeting.

Because the circumstances in each case are different, we will review preparation for calls on existing customers and prospects separately.

Preparing the Meeting

- the first rule is 'always do it'
- think ahead
- work out the structure and sequence
- set clear objectives
- anticipate reactions

Preparation creates a structure, a route map, not a strait-jacket, which will guide you through the meeting. It will not, cannot, anticipate everything that will happen. It is certainly not intended to provide a script. Nor does it restrict your ability to operate creatively, off the cuff where appropriate. It is designed to make being able to do so more straightfor-ward and more likely to be effective.

Existing customers

Planning calls on your existing customers can be comparatively easy: relationships and documentation already exist, from which informa-tion can be drawn to create the basis of your call.

However, even though the relationship and the data in your files will give you a great advantage over a competing newcomer, it's impor-tant that you recognise the essentially *defensive* nature of selling to an existing customer (where you will be 'defending' your product and your relationship from competitor activity), compared to the essentially *offensive* nature of selling to a prospect (where you will be the one 'attacking' to win the prospect's business from his current supplier). Planning an effective defence against predators is as important as planning an attack on your competitors' customers.

There are nine main factors you should consider when planning a call on an existing customer.

The customer's buying record

What has been purchased, when, in what quantities and to what value? Look at the customer's payment record: are any invoices outstanding? Are you still liable for any returns (up-lifted, or sale or return stock)? Are the people involved in the customer's decision-making process (which may well involve several people) the same; are the policies the same; are the influences on purchase decisions the same? Think about the customer's current circumstances and plans: is his potential order a regular order to replenish stock (a straight repeat purchase), or might it be a modified repurchase (i.e. he wants a product variant), or might it be a completely new purchase to satisfy his business development plans? What happened last time?

The overall objectives and resources

What are the product mix, volume, value and penetration targets for your territory? What are the available sales aids (for your use and those designed as leave-behinds for customers or end users)? Is your call supported by advertising and/or merchandising? What are the campaign dates? Are you fully resourced: product knowledge, demonstration skills, literature, samples, record cards, forward appointments, business cards, etc.?

Call objectives

Do you have all the data needed to create maximum and fall-back call objectives, objectives that are realistic and achievable?

The call opening

Do you know what to say, how to appear, how to behave in order to build on the existing relationship?

The interview

Which interview plan will you use? Have you worked out what questions to ask, and in what sequence? Have you ideas about the customer's needs, and thus how you will resolve them?

Possible objections

What might they be; when might they arise; how will you handle them?

The close

How will you close? (If negotiation – a whole additional area – is involved, what variables are you prepared to concede; which ones are fixed; what must you gain from any negotiation?)

Follow-up

How will you build a link from this call to the next?

Time

With all that you must achieve with this customer at this call, have you worked out a personal time plan, designed to maximise your utilisation of the available working hours?

Clearly, the more facts you know about your existing customers' needs and habits, the more you should be able to answer these planning questions. However, be aware that such knowledge can lead to over-confidence and could blind you to seeing opportunities that a newcomer, with a more inquisitive mind and 'attacking' stance, might spot. In other words, are you sure that you have the complete – and up-to-date – picture concerning every part of your customer's business where one of your products might fit?

Prospects

Obviously, a serious problem with prospects is often the lack of information available about them and, by definition, the lack of a relationship.

Your planning emphasis must therefore be on research and the actual interview opening, which is, it might be argued, more important to the success of a prospect visit than to an existing customer, because the opening moments of a prospect interview create a sharply-defined focus on which the chance of a future relationship depends.

Thus, the more relevant you can make your opening the higher will be your chances of raising your prospect's interest and receptiveness, and of building trust – the very necessary ingredient of empathy. Remember, you may not have more than one chance to get close to a prospect: your first approach, particularly if winning business from a competitor is the prize, must be a good one.

There are four main factors which constitute the research and planning demands for visits to prospects.

● **Desk research on the prospect's** financial status; his markets and customers; specifications; corporate objectives; owners, directors and other key stakeholders; strategic business units; products; processes; plant; employees; unions, etc. This information can be found in the prospect's annual or mid-term financial and shareholders' reports, in relevant business directories and reference books, and so on.

- **Face-to-race research on the prospect's** decision-makers and purchase influencers; buying patterns; current and future needs, etc.

- **Possible call objectives**. These should be detailed as the available pre-call data allows, but remember that your objectives will probably need revision on the spot in the light of your initial meeting.

- **Prospect development** or how to create and develop a relationship which benefits both parties. (You may only be able to plan this after your initial meeting.)

The checklists will help you fill out these principles.

Call planning sales checklists		
Existing customers	**Yes**	**No**
1 Are my *objectives*:		
• stated as customer needs?	——	——
• commercially worth while?	——	——
• consistent with our policy?	——	——
• achievable within our resources?	——	——
• measurable?	——	——
• timed?	——	——
2 Have I done enough *research* on:		
• the person to be seen?	——	——
• the customer situation?	——	——
• recommenders?	——	——

	Yes	No
• influencers?	———	———
• supporters?	———	———
• their needs?	———	———
• competition?	———	———

3 Will my *opening*:
- • put him at ease?   ———   ———
- • get him interested and talking?   ———   ———
- • explore his needs?   ———   ———
- • establish his priorities?   ———   ———

4 Will my *presentation*:
- • offer desirable results from his point of view?   ———   ———
- • prove my case to his satisfaction?   ———   ———
- • explain complex points simply?   ———   ———
- • show how his needs can be met?   ———   ———

5 If he raises *objections*:
- • have I considered what they might be?   ———   ———
- • have I got answers which will satisfy him?   ———   ———
- • are they related to his needs?   ———   ———

6 Will my *close*:
- • get a commitment?   ———   ———
- • match my objectives?   ———   ———
- • make it easy for him to agree?   ———   ———
- • leave him feeling better than before the call?   ———   ———

	Yes	No
7 In terms of *equipment*:		
• have I identified what I will need?	———	———
• have I identified what he may need?	———	———
• have I got it with me?	———	———
• have I decided how to use it?	———	———

Prospects

	Yes	No
1 For *objectives* see checklist on existing customers		
2 Have I done enough *research* on:		
• background information on this prospect?	———	———
– published sources?	———	———
– prospect sources?	———	———
– other sources?	———	———
• background information on his industry?	———	———
– published sources?	———	———
– prospect sources?	———	———
– other sources?	———	———
• background information on his competition?	———	———
– published sources?	———	———
– prospect sources?	———	———
– other sources?	———	———
• possible needs?	———	———
• major needs?	———	———

	Yes	No
• future plans?	———	———
• whether there is an obvious need for my product/services?	———	———
• whether it has sales potential?	———	———
(and see Checklist on existing customers)		

3 Will my *opening*:

	Yes	No
• fill gaps in essential knowledge?	———	———
– buying process?	———	———
– decision-makers?	———	———
– industry situation?	———	———
– company situation?	———	———
– organisation?	———	———
– needs?	———	———
– competition?	———	———
– his?	———	———
– ours?	———	———
• impress him about me?	———	———
• impress him about the company?	———	———
(and see existing customers)		

4 For *presentations* see existing customers

5 For *objections* see existing customers

6 For *close* see existing customers

7 For *equipment* see existing customers

None of this planning is of real use without clear objectives, however, the better the information you have, or have put together, the more precisely you can then set your objectives.

Setting Objectives

There is an old saying which advises 'if you don't know where you are going, any road will do'. So it is with objectives: if you know what the end point is it will help you work back and establish how to get there, how to open, how to tackle each stage.

A call objective must be concise, but nevertheless expressed in the five 'dimensions' represented by the familiar mnemonic SMART (**S**pecific **M**easurable **A**chievable **R**ealistic and **T**imed). That is, a call objective must be:

specific – expressed precisely;

measurable – it must contain a quantified goal against which your performance can be measured;

achievable – it must not be so difficult as to make its achievement beyond your current capabilities, or beyond what your customer/prospect could commit to at this call;

realistic – it must not be so easy that achieving it contributes nothing to the progress of the sale or your relationship with your customer/prospect;

timed – it must contain a time limit by which you will have fulfilled your objective.

Thus, 'Sell Mr Marks 600 widgets' does not express a SMART call objective; nor is 'Get a referral appointment to see Mrs Smith'. These 'statements of intent' could be better expressed SMARTly as:

> To persuade Mr Marks at this visit to take
> 600 widgets plus corresponding spares, and
> give our products a trial in demonstrations
> over a minimum 4 weeks.

> To convince Mr White at this call to refer
> me to Mrs Smith for a 30-minute interview
> today.

These objectives are *specific*, they clearly state *what* must be achieved, *when* they must be achieved, and both contain a *measurement* against which performance can be judged. If we assume that they are also achievable and realistic, such SMART objectives will tie you down to a precise goal and concentrate your energy on what you are at the call to achieve. SMART call objectives will discipline you and minimise unprofitable meandering from the task.

Unfortunately, it does happen that sometimes you make calls when factors you predicted *might* occur, but you hoped never would, actually do occur and prevent you achieving your call objective. Is there any way of minimising this problem of calls that divert sharply from expectations?

One option is to weigh up the new factors and revise your call objectives on the spot, and assume that the revised objective really is the best that you could have achieved in the circumstances. Some sales people can do this, but others find that trying to think constructively and plan a new approach while actually with a buyer may be less than successful, and results in a revised objective that is more of an ego-saver than a genuinely useful business goal.

Another option is to consider potential objective-inhibiting factors during your pre-call planning, and prepare two types of call objective: a *primary* objective and a *secondary* (or fall-back) objective.

A primary objective represents the maximum that is achievable at a call; the ideal. It is the goal that the interview must lead to. It will not necessarily be easy, but if achieved it will be a significant result.

A secondary objective is something less which, if secured, will still progress the sale and enable you to retrieve something of real value from your interview. A pre-planned secondary objective gives you a rational fall-back position for when those unhoped-for factors do occur, and a sound basis from which to negotiate a revised offer, rather than allowing the pressure of the situation to compromise your clear thinking. The strength and confidence you can gain from a pre-determined fall-back position is immeasurable.

Recording objectives

To help you focus on your objectives in the often dynamic exchanges that take place during a sales interview, particularly when it is one in a series of long-term, high-value interviews, you may find it useful to record call objectives on a planning format.

At its simplest, a planning format looks like this:

Customer/Prospect _____
Contact name _____
Date of visit _____
PRIMARY CALL OBJECTIVES
SECONDARY (fallback) OBJECTIVES

For some, planning formats may need to be more comprehensive and include space not only for primary and secondary call objectives but also for notes on other aspects of the meeting.

The complexity of the detail you need to put on the planning format you use will depend on the kind of call you make and the nature of your business. In any event, the principal values of a planning format should be as follows.

- **Discipline** A planning format must be seen as a commitment. You resolve not to walk away from a call until you have secured, as a minimum, the secondary call objective (which you pre-determined would still serve the purpose of your visit, even though it is not the maximum that you could have attained).

- **Focus** If you keep your planning slip literally in your view (though not in your customer's/prospect's), or at least in mind, throughout an interview, you can be sure of never losing sight of what you are at the call to achieve. This may seem to be an obvious point to make; but perhaps there have been times when you have momentarily lost the control of an interview to your customer, or the customer has thrown irrelevant points into the conversation or it has been highly animate – and suddenly you wonder what you are supposed to be doing. A glance at the objectives on your planning slip will refocus your thoughts on to the task at hand and allow you to keep the meeting on track.

- **Revision** Of course there will be times when facts that materially affect your planning objectives only emerge during an interview. If the objectives are written out beforehand, it will be easier for you to revise them – and still maintain realism – than it will be to organise SMART objectives under your contact's gaze.

So to sum up: call objectives provide a target for the meeting. With a defined target to aim for, the interview can be steered towards an intended conclusion. Knowing the end-point means that the sales opening can be planned with great precision.

Remember: do not forget yourself

At this point it is worth mentioning that you should not forget to plan the visible impact you will make on the meeting. Details are all too easy to neglect, and this may be compounded by haste. A conscious effort and decision to match appearance broadly to the prospect's expectations is well worth while.

This involves a number of factors, some practical (someone selling to farmers needs to keep wellington boots in the car), others more to do with image. There is a fine line between a smart suit and a sharp suit. A salesperson can to a degree reflect the prevailing standards of the customer, for example selling to advertising agencies whose employees are all fashionably dressed may mean doing likewise (though not, perhaps, outdoing them!). Common sense is the best guide, and, if in doubt, remain conventional and smart in a professional way. Describing the objective in terms of what competencies you wish to project, rather than simply what appearance you have may help find the right balance; if the prevailing impression needs to be of efficiency, expertise, or one of technical competence, then your appearance must be designed to establish just that. Some salespeople lose important elements of a good first impression because they look 'tatty'. Clearly, being smartly dressed, well turned out and with appropriate attention to detail (clean fingernails and shoes, for instance) are important.

It is equally important that you should project an appearance of efficiency, by which is meant a little more than simply being efficient. For example, your briefcase or sample case should be tidy and well organised. Your calculator should have batteries in, visual aids should be ready, accessible and in the right order. A moment's thought, such as keeping shoe polish in the car, can make small but important differences to appearances. And as Oscar Wilde said, 'It is only shallow people who do not judge by appearances'.

Overall, when a sales meeting turns out well, it rarely has anything much to do with chance (good luck is only useful to explain why your competitors are successful). It is more likely to be because it was well researched, well planned and set up; and subsequently well executed.

A route map for the meeting

Earlier we looked at the decision-making process used by the customer to make buying decisions. We will now relate the seven stages involved to the four main stages of the face-to-face meeting; that is opening, presenting the case, handling objections and closing. This is the real route map, what has to be borne in mind here is not a fixed way forward, but a structure and approach which will guide the way through the conversation, enabling the salesperson to maintain the initiative and yet make what is going on entirely acceptable to the prospect.

The route map analogy is a good one. You have to keep the full picture in front of you and, even if selecting different choices along the route, keep moving in the right direction. In addition, the fine detail is important; miss one signpost and you are off the route and will perhaps be lost. Similarly, the detail is important here, as we move through the four stages. Small – perhaps seemingly basic – details are as important to the success of the whole encounter as the big issues.

Session 3

....

Opening a call

Explain how this opening stage of the sales meeting relates to the first two points on the overall buying/selling process sequence

OPENING A CALL

> I am important.
> Consider my needs.

What are the facts?
What are the snags?
What shall I do?
I approve.

and why it is important to consider the opening from the customers point of view.

Importance of the opening

Emphasise and explain the importance of being able to **lead and direct** the sales interview – running the kind of meeting **we** want and that customers find they like – dealing effectively with the varying customer attitudes that can exist at these early stages.

Emphasise that what happens during the opening moments of the sales meeting could affect the tone of the entire meeting, and the relationship that we build, and could thus influence the outcome of the whole interview.

List the key elements of opening on the flip chart. The list shown provides an agenda for the several important things that must go on during the opening stages (it can be used progressively and referred back to during this session).

OPENING THE SALE

- create interest
- identify needs
- agree needs
- create needs
- establish priorities

Emphasise the importance of the first stage, just establishing interest and attention. This can be done by a combination of:

a greeting

an interest-creating comment

the reason for calling

a (fact-finding) question

and must be orientated to the customer, i.e., not 'I happened to be passing', but 'this will interest you' (and why).

Make a note of examples of real conversation you may wish to quote:

_____

_____

_____

_____

_____

Write the heading 'CUSTOMER NEEDS'.

Explain the importance of **exploring and identifying customer needs**.

Ask the group for ideas on how this could be done.

List them on the flip chart.

You should try to get the following answers:

questions – open (i.e. that cannot be answered 'yes' or 'no') and probing statements
questions and statements in combination.

Explain that you are now going to deal with these in more detail.

Questioning techniques

Explain that there are four basic types of questioning technique, all designed to help us progressively probe and find out what the customer's needs really are.

Draw lines on either side of the flip chart (as shown) to represent the sides of a funnel.

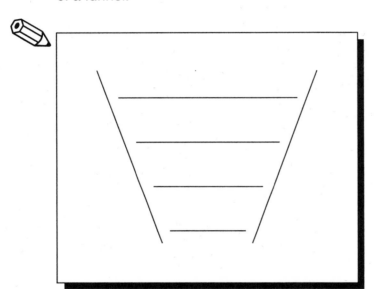

 Write 'BACKGROUND' at the top of the funnel and **explain** that you will deal with this type first and show with the aid of the funnel how it is possible to get closer to the customer's real needs.

Then **read out** an example of a background question relevant to your business. An example – from the printing business – is given with space to record your own example.

'How many corporate brochures do you print in a typical year?'

_____

_____

_____

Ask the group to contribute other examples of background questions.

List good examples on the flip chart.

Write in the neck of the funnel 'PROBLEM' and explain that the second and complementary technique involves asking problem questions.

Relate the next example question to the first background question. In the printing example this can be done by **explaining** that we should assume the answer indicated that the potential customer had a quite high volume of corporate brochures printed in a typical year.

Ask the group to think of a problem question that could be asked next to try and identify if the customer is experiencing any problems.

After you have heard a few contributions **read out** an appropriate example:

(As in the continuing print example:
'Does the volume of corporate brochure work cause you any problems?')

_____

_____

_____

and:

Explain that this is typical of the sort of question that could be asked.

Ask the group for further examples of problem questions they have used or can think of and discuss them briefly. Next:

Write on the flipchart: 'IMPLICATION'.

Continue with the linking process and ask the group what form they think an implication question would take, again asking for examples if necessary:

Suggest the correct response should be something like ...... and **read** it out:

(Print example:
'How does that affect quality at peak times?')

_____

_____

_____

Ask the group for examples of other implication questions and discuss them briefly, then:

Write on the flip chart: 'NEED'.

Again continue with the linking process and, as before, **ask** the group what form they think a need question would take.

The correct response should be something like ......
and **read** it out:

(Print example: 'If we could find a way of working with you to reduce the load, and make sure all the brochures are consistently good, would that help?')

_____

_____

_____

Summarise this section on 'Questioning Techniques' by **explaining** that you will be going through the four questions again, but this time providing a complete example using both sides of the conversation used as an example.

Print example

QUESTIONS	ANSWERS
1 'How many corporate brochures do you print a year?'	'At least a dozen main ones, I suppose.'
2 'Does the volume of corporate brochure work cause you any problems?'	'Well, certainly there are peaks of activity when it gets pretty hectic.'
3 'How does that affect quality at peak times?'	'It sometimes means some are more simply done to leave us free to concentrate on the design of the more complicated ones.'
4 'If we could find a way of working with you to reduce the load, and make sure all the brochures are consistently good, would that help?'	'Anything that eased the problem would be welcome.'

Note that such answers can be useful later in the meeting, allowing the salesperson to refer back linking suggestions to the customer's stated view.

Make a note of any similar example specific to your business:

_____

_____

_____

_____

_____

Explain that in general terms **successful salespeople**:

ask fewer background questions

ask more questions

convert problem and implication questions into **need** questions, and that **unsuccessful sales people** tend to:

ask a large number of background questions

introduce their solution after asking background questions

ask relatively few problem questions

rarely ask implication questions

even more rarely ask need questions

Point out that successful salespeople tend to follow the customer's buying sequence, whilst unsucessful salespeople talk about themselves, their companies and their products, and do so too soon.

This is an important element of the sales process (one which conditions much of what comes next), so to ascertain the principles are clear in people's minds it is worth checking.

Ask participants to select an individual customer and note the answers to the following questions (which might be best listed on the flip chart).

● What do you consider the most important **background information** you will need to have before visiting the customer?

● What **problems** might this customer have which could be alleviated by your product/service?

▶

- If such problems continue what are the **implications**?
- What therefore are these implications stated as **needs**?

Note: this can be dealt with by letting each member of the group work individually on a chosen customer, or by group discussion focusing on a selected customer.

Statement Techniques

Explain that each type of question can have an equivalent statement and that the same sequence can be used as with questions: background/problem/implication/need.

For example, instead of asking:

(Print example: **'How are these unacceptability high costs affecting your business?'**
say: **'Consequently, you're not perhaps able to achieve the margins you need and as a result your prices are on the high side.'**)

or:

_____

_____

_____

Statements can be confidently used when we have a thorough understanding of the customer's situation. They are usually used **after** questioning to reinforce and clarify that both we and the customer have reached the same understanding at a given stage. With practice it is possible to combine questions and statements and so avoid extremes of interrogation and lecture.

The most effective and safest way of using them is to make statements of fact and ask questions about conclusions, e.g., 'In your type of business the chief factors affecting costs are packaging and distribution expenses. Which of them is causing the biggest headache?'

Make a note of any other example of this sequence relating to actual customers:

_____

_____

_____

_____

_____

Agreeing needs

Explain that it is not enough to find out. The customer must be aware that this is happening and agree we are correct. Expressions such as – ' …so that means …' – allowing the customer to confirm – 'Yes, that's right' are useful.

Creating a need

Explain that customers who have definite needs often will buy with very little encouragement.

If customers are satisfied with current (other) suppliers they will need a reason to he dissatisfied before they will consider a change to a new supplier.

If this is very much your situation the point is worth emphasising.

Faced with customers who are satisfied with existing solutions we will have to create dissatisfaction before the customer will consider a change.

The task is to create dissatisfaction **without** criticising the customer's previous buying decisions – as this will make him defensive.

The best method for doing this is to show that the situation is unsatisfactory, due to factors outside the customer's control.

Summarise the main sequence on the flip chart.

CREATING A NEED

Reason for dissatisfaction
↓
Create dissatisfaction
(without criticism)
↓
Factors outside customers control
↓
Acceptable new solution

Ask the group to think of factors which might cause such dissatisfaction and are outside the customer's control which could be particularly relevant to them and the type of potential customer they meet.

List relevant contributions on the flip chart. Some examples are shown.

Bad delivery record

Bad advice (from the salesperson)

High cost

Not getting value for money

Poor design standards

Not meeting the brief

Changes made without consultation

Rather as with the way it was suggested some debate on focusing on needs was just handled:

Ask participants (perhaps with the same customer in mind) to imagine a wrong action/decision being made and then note the answers to the following (which might be displayed on the flip chart):

- What was the **wrong action**?
- What **negative effects** could it be producing for the customer?
- What factors (outside the customer's control) might be **blamed**?
- How do the **cause – effects** – and a **possible solution** link?

This may be worth open discussion for a few minutes.

Establishing priorities

Explain that customers will normally have a variety of needs, and they will rarely all be of equal importance, indeed they may clash in the way, say, time and cost often do.

It is, therefore, essential that we not only establish the customer's needs but also his priorities.

This is usually done with simple questions.

Summarise by getting the customer to state his needs during the opening of the sales meeting. The salesperson is able to get to know the criteria by which the customer will judge his proposition. He can then select those aspects of the proposition that will have the greatest appeal to the customer.

Ask for any questions from the group before proceeding.

TIME:

BACKGROUND NOTES

Opening a call

It is a funny thing about meetings; you may have noticed that they have two beginnings. One is ritual. It is concerned with the initial remarks such as 'Good morning', but also 'Did you find our offices OK?', 'What a dreadful day, nothing but rain the whole summer' (so what else is new?). Remarks like this allow us to get into the swing of things. Then, someone, often the buyer, says something like, 'Right, what I suggest we do this morning is . . .', and the meeting starts again. You know the feeling.

This area is worthy of consideration, but with care we are, after all, only talking about a minute or two and must not get ridiculously psychological about it (certainly it takes longer to review than actually to happen). But it is important. We want to run and direct the meeting. Not in an unpleasant sense from the point of view of the customer; the trick is to *run the kind of meeting you want and the customer finds he likes* (and preferably likes more than any meetings he has with your competitors). Only one person can effectively be 'in charge'. There is a line in Shakespeare's *Much Ado about Nothing* that says when 'Two men ride of a horse, one must ride behind'. This certainly makes the point. If the salesperson does not get hold of the meeting the customer surely will. So, what can we do about this?

The answer lies in those first, ritual moments. Unless, the initiative is taken then, it may not be possible to take it for some time; at worst it will be completely lost. Specifically, this means keeping the conversation off the weather or whatever and contributing something more businesslike which still fulfils the ritual process. The two tactics outlined below make good examples.

Appeal to pride

When using this tactic you comment on something positive about the customer's business. This could be simply an observation of how smart his new reception area looks, 'I'm sure it impresses all your customers', or may come from your research, 'I noticed in last week's trade papers how successful you have been with the export initiative in the Far East'. Good research will mean you know your customer will be able to say, 'Yes, I'm very pleased about that'. This kind of comment shows an interest, it shows you have done some checking and it provides a ritual moment of *relevant* conversation.

Good turns

This approach is very effective with people you see regularly.

A good exponent of the 'good turn' approach is a salesperson who comes to see me regularly. He notes the kind of work I do, the kind of industries I work in and will often arrive with, say, a magazine article in his briefcase. 'I know you do a lot in the hotel and travel industry,' he might say, 'I wondered if you had seen this?' Seen it or not, I like the approach and it often produces something interesting. It costs him, of course, nothing except a little time and attention.

Many similar actions can be taken, and then the salesperson can move on to say 'Let's get down to business', from which control of the meeting follows more naturally.

At the same time the beginning of the opening should flow through a structure, if only to avoid starting with the trite phrases of the less professional salesperson: 'I just happened to be passing'; 'How's business?' and so on.

POINT

> ## Direction
>
> - take the initiative
> - lead the meeting
> - make the customer feel this is natural and right
>
> Getting hold of the meeting, being in charge, makes an excellent start to the proceedings. Run the kind of meeting you want and which they find they like – and preferably like better than anything being done by your competitors.
>
> Start off in charge; stay in charge.

The elements to be orchestrated at the beginning are:

A greeting + an interest-creating comment + the reason for calling

plus

either a check for any outstanding issues *or* the first fact-finding question

The greeting

Obviously, your greeting must be right for the time of day but also for the depth of your relationship and your customer's/prospect's personality type. This means that even long-standing customers can still expect a formal greeting, whereas some prospects respond well to an informal greeting. In any doubt, take the formal route.

The question of whether and when to use first names can only be answered within the context of what your company recommends and what each contact finds acceptable. First name use is more common now, but if in doubt remain more, rather than less, formal.

To make it just a little more likely that you will be remembered (after all the prospect may see many different salespeople), when it comes to introducing yourself it is best to use both your names – John Smith – and, at the same time, hand over a business card if you are meeting for the first time.

The interest-creating comment

There are two reasons for including in your opening words an interest-creating comment:

- to demonstrate your knowledge of and interest in your customer's/prospect's industry, company, people, plans, policies, etc.;
- to begin the process of raising the contact's interest in and level of receptivity to you and what you are there for.

The reason for calling

This must be expressed as a buyer benefit. If a relationship already exists between you and a customer you should be easily able to devise a highly relevant benefit; if there is no relationship you must choose a benefit which experience tells you that most customers have found valuable. For instance, with a regular customer the objective may be linked to selling the range, introducing products the customer has not, as yet, tried. If the product shows, let us say, a cost saving in his production, then the benefit is the greater cost benefits of extending his use of the product range. The customer is not likely to be interested in buying more of the range simply because he likes you. This kind of thinking needs to come over, whichever customer is being approached .

A check for outstanding issues

In some industries, for example book publishing or healthcare, it is common practice for a supplier to take back unsold products.
It may well be the best approach to encourage a customer to raise this, or other such outstanding matters, before you begin your current presentation, particularly when returns can be expected. This helps 'clear the decks'. If your customer's priority need is to resolve a problem concerning, say, current stock, this will be in the forefront of his or her mind. Until this need is satisfied he or she will not be receptive to the idea of buying new stock.

In such a case, helping your customer at the outset of an interview may give you some sort of minor bargaining chip; his initial view of you is then more positive.

The first fact-finding question

This is the bridge which links the interview opening with the interview proper. Your question should relate to the interest-creating comment and your reason for calling.

The following examples illustrate the four parts of an opening in action.

Example 1

Greeting	'Hello John. Good to see you again.'
Interest-creating comment	'I see that your company are moving into the DIY field as well.'
Reason for calling	'I'm sure we can help you stay ahead ... even attract *new* customers ... by brightening up the presentation of your displays – especially in the cut wood and garden paving areas.'

First fact-finding question	'Have you seen out new range of outdoor racking?'

Example 2

Greeting	'Good afternoon Dr Smith. John Brown from XYZ Healthcare. Thank you for seeing me. Your receptionist said you've had a busy surgery, so I'll be brief.'
Interest-creating comment	'As you know, this is the time of year when patients presenting with seasonal allergies can significantly increase the workload on health centres.'
Reason for calling	'We're introducing a new care pack which we believe will help ease the burden on GPs and nursing staff, and make patient management simpler and less expensive.'
First fact-finding question	'Could I begin by asking you about the number of patients presenting with [diseases] that you've seen this week?'

Example 3

Greeting	'Good morning Mr Jones. I hope you had a good holiday. You certainly seem to have found the sun.'
Interest-creating comment	'I know you've had tremendous success with your new children's section; in fact, your assistant said you were already thinking of expanding your range of teenage titles.'
Reason for calling	'It's the classics that are enjoying renewed popularity, as you know; and we're launching a new imprint starting with seven of the all-time best. They could create what you're looking for: a focal point to attract more childrens' sales.

A check for outstanding issues	'Before we take a closer look at out lead titles, do you have any returns you'd like me to handle for you?'

Example 4

Greeting	'Hello there, James; how are you?'
Interest-creating comment	'I have got together the details about service arrangements you asked for when I was here last week.'
Reason for calling	'It should only take 15/20 minutes to go through them together and see how they will work with your production schedule.'
First fact-finding question	'Did you get out the schedules we discussed?'

Of course, this is not a set routine. There may be a more dramatic way of creating an impact and getting a hearing. I once met a particular airline representative. One of his jobs was to call on travel agents and brief many members of their staffs, updating them on schedules, fares etc. Traditionally this was done by moving round the office talking to each in turn. It worked but was time-consuming. With certain bigger accounts he had another approach.

He arrived, from a nearby sandwich shop, with a tray of coffee and doughnuts. He was able to gather the majority of the staff around him for a coffee break and later pick up individually the odd ones left manning the phones. It worked well, and the 'doughnut-man' achieved good co-operation from his major accounts. Every business needs thinking about in terms of how such individual, and distinctive, impact can be made.

This idea will not, of course, be right for everyone. It does, however, demonstrate the right kind of thinking; such an approach may prompt other ideas. Other approaches are more generally applicable. Suggesting, for example, an agenda can help you get hold of the meeting. An agenda that suits you, but also makes sense to the customer, and is phrased carefully: 'It might be most helpful to you, Mr Customer, if we were to take . . . first, then . . .'. This is a good example of sales technique coming over to the customer as helpful and focusing on his needs. He is at liberty to amend your suggestion, but you are both likely to end up following broadly your suggestion.

Having made a good start, there is still a great deal going on in the opening stages of the sale. Perhaps the most important is concerned with finding out about customers and their needs.

Identification of customer needs

Customer attitudes vary at the beginning of interviews. They can be friendly, hostile, indifferent, interested, helpful or defensive. The opening of an interview is a crucial time for both parties.

Remember the first two steps in the systematic way people approach any buying decision outlined in the previous chapter:

- I am important and want to be respected
- Consider my needs.

These two steps make the salesperson's objectives at the beginning of an interview very clear:

- to make a customer feel important in the salesperson's eyes (to which the preliminaries contribute) and
- to agree to the customer's stated needs.

Successful selling is particularly dependent on this stage in the process being well handled. Exploring and identifying the customer's needs correctly makes him want to hear your propostion. Subsequently, making it attractive reduces the possibility of objections and thus obtains more voluntary commitment.

Remember, people act to relieve a felt need. Where the need, is low, the solution has a high impact, either positively or negatively, depending on the way it is offered. Sometimes customers will volunteer their needs clearly. More often, needs have to be explored, identified and spelt out before we can move on.

◯INT

Identifying needs

- ask the right questions, in the right way
- be more precise and thorough than your competitors in finding out what the customers really want
- find out their real reasons for these needs

It is not putting it too strongly to suggest that this is a 'sheep and goats' factor in selling. That is, those who find out more about client needs, and are seen to do so by the client, have a head start on everything else that follows.

Get a firm basis of information; it can be the first step to beating competition.

Exploration can be carried out by either questions or statements, or by a combination of both questions and statements. Questions are initially safer and more productive, but they have to be carefully and correctly used. The precise method of questioning technique most likely to bring results utilises four basic types of question, which are used in sequence to probe for more information – and information of a less general nature that is more focused on what the customer really wants and why. The four types of question you can use are as follows.

Background questions

For example, 'What's your unit cost per item?'

Problem questions

For example, 'Are unit costs a problem?'

Implication questions

For example, 'What effect are high unit costs having on the rest of the business?'

Need questions

For example, 'What would you like to happen as far as unit costs are concerned?'

Open or closed questions can be equally successful, but open questions (ones that cannot be answered with a 'yes' or 'no') encourage the client to talk and produce more information.

The type and combination of questions used is very important. Experience shows that asking fewer background questions but focusing them better, asking more problem questions, amplifying problems by asking implication questions, and converting problems and implications into need questions works best and forms a logical sequence. On the other hand asking a relatively large number of background questions, fewer problem, implication or need questions, and introducing solutions after the stage of asking background questions works less well.

The reason for this difference is simple. The first sequence follows the customer's buying sequence, while the latter makes salespeople talk about themselves, their firms and their products/services, which distances the approach from the customer.

Each type of question also has an equivalent approach based on a statement for which the same sequence can be used. This is background – problems – implication – needs, and statements can be most confidently used when there is already a thorough understanding of the customer's situation. Thus, they are more often used after questioning or during subsequent meetings.

Customers with strongly felt needs will often buy with very little encouragement. Many, however, are satisfied with existing solutions. Faced with this situation then we must, in fact, create some dissatisfaction before the customer will consider a change. (This is explored in more detail when we look at *Creating (or extending) needs*, see page 78.)

A final point about questioning: you do not just have to ask questions, you have to *listen* to the answers; and what you do next should be based on those answers. If you proceed apparently as if you had not heard, and the prospect feels they are hearing the 'standard pitch', something that bears no relation to their spoken requirements, you will naturally not be so well received.

Listening

- listen very carefully
- concentrate on listening
- take note of what is said
- be seen to be a good listener
- adapt what you plan to do in light of what you hear

This is very simple (at least to state). Good salespeople are good listeners. It is said that mankind was created with two ears and one mouth and that should be a reflection on their use. It is very easy to find that we are not listening – really listening – to customers.

Listen actively and note the information you obtain.

Agreeing needs

Discovering customer needs, while it may be an important step, is not all that needs to be done. While knowing what the customer wants, and why he wants it, will help; if the information is obtained in a way which makes it clear to the customer exactly what you know – this will do more. The customer must know you know, and this is important; it implies *agreement* of needs. What does this mean in practice? Well, that you do not just say to yourself, as perhaps a print salesman might, 'so he is interested in quality work'. Nor is it sufficient if you discover why, 'because promotional print has an impact on his customers'. On such key issues this has to be checked back. The customer must be asked, 'It is not just quality work you are after in an academic sense, it is something that will guarantee the right impact on your customers, is that right?'. If the answer is affirmative you know you are on target. It may also be more useful later to refer back to this in a way that recaps, '*You did say impact on customers was the important thing*', rather than suggest, 'It seems to me therefore that what you want is . . .'.

So, can you now move on to presenting your case, sure that everyone's needs are understood and agreed? Sorry, no; there is still more to be done before the opening stage is complete.

Creating (or extending) needs

As the conversation progresses, there may be an opportunity to *create* needs. Sometimes this is done by helping customers discover needs of which they were unaware. More often it can involve suggesting that marginal differences in need are better met by your product or service than by that of someone else. In this case it may be necessary to create dissatisfaction with an existing supplier; And this must be done carefully. If not, it will be seen as critical of the customer's previous buying decisions, this will be resented and, at worst, may lead to an argument.

Rather, the salesperson will have to show that the situation is unsatisfactory due to factors outside the customer's control by mentioning, for example, such factors as:

- other suppliers' poor delivery record
- other suppliers' bad service
- poor design standards.

In addition, questioning will often identify hidden, unstated needs, sometimes beyond an initially stated position.

With that in mind, there is still one more thing involved in the opening stage.

Establishing priorities

Customers often have a mix of needs. This is not surprising, especially when technical or complex products or services are being bought. As questioning reveals the needs it may well be that conflicts become apparent: 'I want this delivered immediately, tailored to our requirements and at the lowest possible quote'. All these factors may be possible, individually, but which is most important?

Early delivery may be possible with items from a standard range, and this may meet the need reasonably well. But will it be well enough? If the buyer really wants a tailored solution, is he prepared to wait for delivery? And so on and so on. There may be a neat list of three key priorities, or a complex picture of many different factors to be taken into account. In either case the principle is the same: we have to try to sort out the customer's priorities, not simply form a view of what the priorities would be for most customers (much less what *we* think they should be). Again, this adds to our information base and can be of great use as the meeting progresses, guiding us towards the right presentation, one that reflects the customer's priorities.

So far so good

At the end of the opening stage what sort of view should the customer have of the salesperson? Assume that they have never met before. The initial impressions are important. The immediate view should be of someone professional: that is well turned out, getting down to business positively, having an instant customer orientation, likely to know what he is talking about, well organised and, overall, worth giving a hearing.

The opening stage should build on this first view. As it progresses, then to the above should be added a feeling that the way the salesperson is working is tailored to the customer, in other words what is being said is 100 per cent appropriate; evidence that the salesperson is appreciating, understanding and getting to grips with the customer's point of view; and perhaps, as appropriate to the kind of business involved, they are:

- technically competent
- numerate
- avoiding inappropriate jargon
- creative
- prepared to listen

and, very important, the customer must feel the salesperson is are interested in him and, ideally, is interesting to deal with.

Session 4

....

Presenting your case

Explain that this section deals with the way you want the main presentation to be delivered by the sales team.

It covers how the we can satisfy the needs and priorities of the customer (already established during the opening) with the product/service we offer.

At this stage in the selling process the customer will be wanting to know:

- if the ideas on offer will be of any help to him
- what the facts are.

PRESENTING YOUR CASE

I am important.
Consider my needs.

What are the facts?
What are the snags?

What shall I do?
I approve.

Explain that this can be a delicate balancing process matching the needs of the customer with the services being offered. A 'weighing-up' analogy is a good one; this can be illustrated on the flip chart.

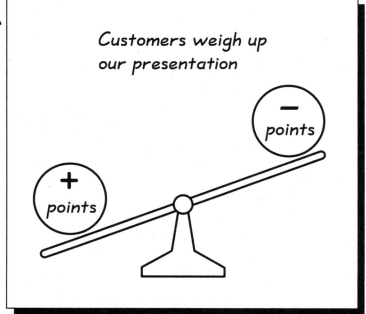

Explain that in delivering this main part of the presentation we have four main objectives.

Our ideas must be:

1 Understandable
2 Attractive
3 Convincing

and in order to know that these three have been achieved we need to obtain:

4 Feedback

 List the four on the flip chart and:

Explain that these will be considered in turn (the list could remain visible while you do so).

Making ideas understandable

It may be useful to start this section off by carrying out a brief communications game: e.g.

Ask participants to draw a line about two inches long on a piece of paper.

Then **ask** them to write the first and last letter of their first name at each end of the line.

When they have done this, **ask** participants what letters they have put at either end of the line.

You should find that – taking the name Patrick as an example – most of the group have put 'P' at one end and 'K' at the other end, i.e.

P_____K

Explain that if they think back to what you **actually** asked, namely to write the first **and** last letter of your surname at each end of the line, what they should have done was to put 'PK' at both ends of the line, i.e.

PK_____PK

Ask the group why they think this occurred.

They may say that they:

- did not listen properly
- made assumptions
- saw a logic in the P_____K answer.

Explain that the real reason for failure was **your** fault. It was a poor piece of communication – witness their failure to do what you wanted. **It is always for the communicator to make things clear**. More sales are lost perhaps because a customer or prospect is unclear than for any other reason. You may like to suggest a example of likely confusion from your own company circumstances.

Make a note of a suitable example:

_____

_____

_____

_____

_____

 Ask for more such examples. It is an important point to get over.

Summarise by saying that the main aim of the game was to show that good communication is not always as easy as we assume – indeed understanding can easily be diluted because this is handled in the belief that we automatically make things in our technical/specialist area clear.

Explain that this part of the course is designed to help participants communicate their ideas and proposals more effectively.

Explain that in order to make his ideas understandable the salesperson needs to:

1 **Structure** the presentation around the customer's needs.

2 Where appropriate **use visual aids** because information presented with them is easier to **understand** and **remember**. It is important to remember that they should be tailored to the customer's individual requirements as much as possible.

3 **Talk the customer's** language by:
- using terms and words which are easily understandable by the customer
- avoiding words or terms which can be misinterpreted.

Discuss the above points in terms of your own organisation's experience.

Make a note of any relevant examples:

_____

_____

_____

_____

Making ideas attractive

Explain (carefully – this is a curiously difficult concept for people to apply) the difference between features and benefits.

_____

_____

_____

_____

and:

Discuss the concept, allowing individual practice until such benefit orientated description is reliably and fluently produced by all.

Making ideas convincing

Stress the importance of being able to substantiate the benefits that are
being communicated to the customer (in other words the salesperson – who
has an axe to grind – saying it is good may need support).

Such substantiation can be added in two ways:

1 by the features which produce them (as you have already demonstrated)

2 by reference to third parties, which are worth a word.

Expain four rules for using third party references:

- use only to **support** our case, **not** as arguments.
- if named they should be respected by the listener.
- the customer and third party should face similar conditions.
- don't just mention the third party – inform the customer of the **benefits**
  that the third party obtained.

Obtaining feedback

Emphasise that we need continuous feedback to ensure that progress is
being made towards our objective. He needs to know

- that he is discussing the customer's real needs.
- if there is a problem in the way the presentation is being presented
- that the proposition is attractive, clear and convincing
- that no key factors have been overlooked

Explain that feedback can be obtained in three main ways:

1 By observation of the customer

2 By waiting and listening to the customer's reply

3 By asking for a comment

Ask the group for suggestions about what to look for when observing a customer during a sales meeting.

Write 'OBSERVATIONS' on a new flip chart sheet. and **list** the group's contributions.

You will want to list **negative factors**: e.g.

● customer repeatedly asking the same question
● looking out of the window
● finger tapping
● looking repeatedly at watch

and **positive** ones, e.g.

● words/expressions that indicate interest and understanding
● watching sales person as he talks
● leaning forward
● nodding.

Conclude this section by reinforcing the following five rules for an effective sales presentation:

1 Take one point at a time.

2 Tell the customer what it means to him in terms of results (talk benefits).

3 Show the customer what it is or means (be descriptive/use illustrations – visual aids).

4 Provide proof where necessary.

5 Check progress by obtaining constant feedback.

This final summary list could usefully go on the flip chart.

TIME:

BACKGROUND NOTES

Presenting your case

This second stage of the face-to-face meeting is the core of the whole sales process.

Once needs are identified and priorities established, the next step is to show how satisfaction will come from the specific products/services or recommendations that are offered. Again the action springs from the appropriate stage of the buying process. If we remember the seven-points involved in a decision to buy, the customer's mental demands are now:

- Will your ideas help me?
- What are the snags?

This means that the salesperson has four objectives as he presents his case: to make his ideas understandable, attractive and convincing (this is what we mean by *persuasive*), and to get feedback that the first three objectives have been achieved.

Each of these elements must be considered in turn and then deployed together in a cohesive and effective conversation.

Making ideas understandable

This is the basis of all communication, and it is especially important in *persuasive* communication. Now, of all the things you do in selling, the core process of telling people about your product or service is the one you no doubt feel you do best. Whatever else, people understand you. Or do they? Communication is never as straightforward as it might seem. Misunderstandings occur all too easily and clarity must be achieved before persuasion is possible. Achieving clarity should not be taken for granted; a mistake which can easily be made as you relate something you know well and deal with regularly.

Without taking due care, however, you may find someone saying 'What do you mean?' in response to something you have said. Sometimes you initiate the correction, 'But I meant . . .', and sometimes, too, people will say to you 'You want me to do *what*?', because, as has been said, communication is not always as easy as it seems; and this shows itself in a number of ways.

It can suffer from being unclear '. . . you fit the thingy on to that sprocket thing and . . .', i.e. just try it, or imprecise '. . . then it's about a mile', i.e. three miles later . . .. It can be so full of jargon that we find ourselves saying manual excavation device, instead of spade. Or it can be gobbledegook:, 'Considerable difficulty has been encountered in the selection of optimum materials and experimental methods, but this problem is being attacked vigorously and we expect the development phase will proceed at a satisfactory rate.' (i.e. we are looking at the handbook and trying to decide what to do.) So much so that the sense is diluted. There are innumerable barriers to communication, not least the assumptions, prejudices and inattention of those on the receiving end.

All this may simply cause a bit of confusion, and take a moment to sort out, or it can cause major problems either immediately or later. But there is never more likely to be problems than when there is an intention to get someone to *do* something, i.e. to buy from you. At least as many sales are probably lost simply because the customer is not clear about what, exactly what, the salesperson means, as are ever lost for any other reasons. It is an area that is worth giving some thought and consideration. What helps to make communication clear? Three factors are key, they are as follows.

Structure and sequence

Presentations should always be structured around the customer's needs. Here is an example. 'So in choosing a system, your first concern is compatibility, your second is simplicity, and your third is productivity. Let's look at the compatibility aspect first, and then deal with the others . . .' You cannot, frankly, label things in advance too often. Such an approach keeps the flow of the argument clear and organised. It is also important to conclude one aspect before moving to the next and to take matters in a logical order.

Visual aids

People understand and remember more when information is presented in visual form. Charts, diagrams, slides, pictures and brochures can all strengthen the clarity of the presentation. In using them follow the basic rules, keep them hidden until they are needed, keep quiet while they are being examined (people cannot concentrate properly on two things at once) and remove them after use to avoid any distraction. Customers like it too if some of the material has clearly been produced specially for your meeting with them.

Jargon

Every company and industry, particularly if its products are technical, has its own language or jargon. Some jargon can be useful, if pitched at the right level, but overall the presentation must use the customer's language. This means using words and terms you are certain the customer understands, and avoiding words or terms which can be misinterpreted in any way, e.g. 'our product is cheap', 'we have a fragmented range of services . . .'.

In a technical business, the aspect of making things understood, clearly understood, can be easily overlooked (you may feel you need some help in making things more persuasive, but surely not simply in explaining the firm, its services or a particular approach). Make sure you really do explain clearly. Many prospects are lost solely because they are confused.

Clarity

- make what you say immediately understandable
- make explanations thorough and precise
- beware of jargon

If the customer cannot understand you there is no way you will be found persuasive. Never underestimate the difficulty of clear communication, even on topics you know well, and remember that anything technical will compound the problem. Get this right and, at best, you will be seen to be a ray of light among those who are less easy to follow. In every contact it will give you a clear run at all the other things you are trying to do.

Think about how to make things clear; clarity will create a foundation for persuasiveness.

Making ideas attractive

People buy things for what they will do for them, or mean to them. It is the desirable results from the buyer's point of view (benefits) that are important, not what things are (features).

Often products or services can do many different things for customers, and not all customers want the same things done. Thus, only those benefits which meet the listener's needs should be mentioned, and it is the process of selecting and matching items from the total list of benefits to an individual customer's specific requirements that makes a particular idea, or solution, appear attractive.

There are normally three types of benefit which can be used: benefits to the listener in his job, or as a person, or benefits to others in which he is interested. The choice will depend on the listener's needs and priorities, though they are not mutually exclusive, as something may affect all three to a similar degree.

This benefit-oriented basis of description in talking with customers is vital. It is another 'sheep and goats' factor. The most successful salespeople do not sell products and services – they sell benefits; that is what customers want to buy. But what, exactly, are benefits? This is worth a moment's careful consideration.

Benefits are what products or services do for the customer. What they are is not important but what they do or mean for the customer is. To take an everyday example, a person does not buy an electric drill because he wants an electric drill, but because he wants to be able to make holes. He buys holes, not a drill. He buys the drill for what it will do (make holes), and this in turn may only be important to him because of a need for storage and a request to put up shelving.

Realising this not only makes selling more effective but also easier. You do not have to describe the same thing in the same way to a lot of different people, but meet each person's needs with potential benefits.

Benefits are what the product or service you sell can do for each individual customer – the things he wants them to do for him. Different customers buy the same thing for different reasons. It is important therefore to identify and use the particular benefits of interest to each. What a product 'does' is described by its benefits.

If this is forgotten, then the things which are important to a customer will not always be seen to be important from the salesperson's viewpoint. The result can, understandably, be a conflict of priorities with the customer focusing on one thing, while the salesperson focuses on the opposite.

The customer is most unlikely to see things from the salesperson's point of view. Each person is, to himself, the most important person in the world. Therefore, to be successful, the salesperson has to be able to see things from the customer's point of view, and demonstrate through his words and actions that he has done so. His chances of success are greater if he can understand the needs of the people he talks to and make them realise that he can fulfil those needs.

This is achieved essentially by the correct use of benefits. In presenting any proposition to a customer, even simply recommending something in reply to a query, you should always translate what you are offering into what it will do.

Often a firm grows introspective and product oriented (this is then all too often reflected in their product literature) and development can reinforce this attitude by adding more and more features. It is only a small step before everyone is busy trying to sell on features alone.

When competitors are almost identical in their performance – at least from a prospect's viewpoint it can be difficult to sell benefits, since all suppliers seem to offer the same benefits. Choice then often depends on the personal appeal of the benefits in those features, rather than on the features themselves. Features are only important if they support the benefits the customer is interested in.

Deciding to concentrate on describing benefits is only half the battle, however. They have to be the right benefits. In fact, benefits are only important to a customer if they describe the satisfaction of his needs. Working out his needs, and then his benefits, means being 'in your customer's shoes'.

There are three types of benefit you can mention:

- benefits to the customer **in his job**, e.g. 'Order processing errors will be eliminated'

- benefits to your customer **as a person**, e.g. 'It will stop people complaining to you about order processing errors'

- benefits to **others in whom the customer is interested**, among colleagues, family, friends, etc., e.g. 'Customers will get the goods that they order'.

Which benefits are the most important? Again, the answer is those that fit in best with your customer's strategic and emotional needs, though they are not, of course, mutually exclusive.

When you think about your proposals you will be able to identify many benefits that can be derived from them; but beware of using too many, believing that the more you use, the more attractive your proposals become. The old saying, 'It's too good to be true' applies here. Too many benefits begin to stretch your customer's credulity.

You can, however, make your benefits more effective by *combining them in a logical sequence* so that, finally, your customer's need is met, e.g. 'With this computerised shelf allocation system, the best assortment of products is fitted into the space available [benefit]. This means that you get continuous sales of the high-volume lines [benefit] while making good margins on the slower movers [benefit]. Generally you optimise sales and profits from the available space, whatever it may be [benefit and need satisfaction]!'

To know what benefits to put forward, you must understand the needs of the buyer to whom you sell and the organisation he represents. Firms often have more than one decision-maker, so it is essential to pinpoint your contact within the hierarchy in order to relate to him accurately.

Typical roles within the decision-making process

Users of service

- may initiate
- may specify
- may veto.

Influencers

- may help specify
- may provide 'expert' objective opinion and information
- may be outsiders
- may be involved in setting criteria for judging between alternative suppliers.

Buyers

- the unit that has formal authority to buy, or has an important influencing role on the decision to buy
- may be measured on the primarily financial aspects (e.g. prices, discounts).

Deciders

- may be the buyers
- may be the end-users
- are frequently the senior members of the end-user department
- may well be the people who control the budget for the service.

Gatekeepers

- those who control the flow of information (or lack of it) to others
- may have the role of an influencer, a buyer or a decider.

To be sure of maximising the strength 'talking benefits' gives to what you say it is useful to analyse products/services in terms of features and benefits, as follows:

Benefit	Feature
Has the ability to dispense tea and coffee simultaneously	Twin, 10-pint, heated containers (equipment for the catering trade)
Gives more miles per gallon	Five-speed gearbox (motor car)
Easier and more comfortable (and perhaps therefore more productive) to use	Ergonomic controls (machine tool)
Provides a quicker, more certain analysis with less disruption of the accounts department	Computer-assisted audit (accountant)

Such an analysis (and it is a useful exercise to work this out point by point) will help differentiate between features and benefits. It is a useful ploy to present the benefits first; because where features lead, i.e. 'we can offer a computer-assisted audit', the customer response (mentally if not spoken) can too often be 'so what?'.

An analysis can be produced for any product or service, or for a range, and can be presented within a company to help everyone learn just what is a feature and what is a benefit. If this is done you produce a checklist, a prompt to conversation which will help lead you into the right kind of *descriptive* presentation.

The power of description can then be extended by relating benefits, different benefits, to the different people involved in the decision. For example, the rugged design of a computerised order processing system might mean:

Increased operator output and reduced fatigue	a benefit . . . to the supervisor
Improved levels of customer service, better company image and more repeat buying	a benefit . . . to the sales office manager
Saves cost, on maintenance and replacement	a benefit . . . to the financial manager

Such a format can be designed and used for each product/service, and any number of people across the decision-making process.

Note that not all the needs will be objective ones; most buyers also have subjective requirements bound up in their decisions. Even with technical things the final decisions can sometimes be heavily influenced by subjective factors, perhaps seemingly of minor significance, once all the objective needs have been met.

By matching benefits to individual customer's needs, you are more likely to make a sale, for the benefits must match a buyer's needs.

Involvement and demonstration

It has long been said of selling motor cars that the most important step is for the salesperson to get the prospect to sit in the driver's seat. It is a manifestation of that Americanism, 'ownership', but the lesson is clear; get the prospect to imagine the product or service in use and you will certainly be that much nearer to a sale.

This points back to what we have already mentioned about being descriptive (an element of 'talking benefits') but also involves physical involvement. A couple of examples perhaps illustrate the point.

Take a demonstration first. If a piece of equipment is being demonstrated, say, a word processing typewriter, then clearly the salesperson has to be able to demonstrate it effectively. He does not have to type fast, but he does have to be able to set up the machine, be familiar with the controls, be able to answer questions and so on. Further, he should be able to explain clearly and know how to get the prospect sitting at the keyboard experiencing the machine's excellence for him or herself. This means being able to guide them, and setting things up individually either for the experienced typist or the person with limited keyboard skills. All this applies even more if what is being demonstrated is more technical, complex or difficult to handle.

Demonstrations have to go right. If the prospect is left saying to himself, 'Even the sales person finds it difficult', he is hardly likely to buy.

A second example comes from the meetings industry. A conference organiser is looking round a hotel. He stands just inside the door of the room suggested for his planned event. The room is empty (or, sometimes, contains the last, messy, remnants of what went on there the previous day), and the salesperson points out the features. He lists the individually controllable lights, the good acoustics, the easy way in which equipment can be brought in and set up and so on. Alternatively, the conference buyer is taken right into the room. He is not told about the acoustics, they are demonstrated as the salesperson speaks to him from the far end of the room, he is offered the opportunity to try out his slides, and he is taken to stand on the verandah where the morning break can be taken. Such an experience lets the person 'live' *their* event, imagine it happening – successfully – in that hotel, that room. It is not, or should not be, the standard tour but is tailored to the person instead. An organising secretary will be made especially familiar with the reception area, and aspects of the meeting with which they will be involved.

A conference speaker will be encouraged to see how he feels on the platform. If the room can be laid out, even in part, as it will be on the day, so much the better.

In this way the prospect literally begins to take part in the selling process and can leave the demonstration able to say 'I *know* it will work'.

OINT

Talking benefits

- understand the difference between features and benefits
- select the benefits appropriate to each customer
- lead with benefits

Talking benefits is always a basic component of an effective sales approach; it translates the case into customer terms and makes it absolutely clear you are seeing things from the customer's point of view. Check you are doing it justice; all your briefing and much of your thinking about your company and its products/services will be introspective, and may prompt an introspective view and approach, unless you do so.

Tell customers what is in it for them.

Knowing how and why customers view you and your organisation as they do is a prerequisite to improving all the specific communication areas reviewed here and to making your own use of them more effective.

Making ideas convincing

If benefits are claims for the product/service, they may have to be substantiated, as sales claims are always viewed with some scepticism. This can be done by describing the features which produce them, or by reference to third parties.

Third party references must be used only to support the case, not as arguments in themselves. If a specific third party is named it should be one respected by the listener (probably not a competitor), and it should face similar conditions to the customer. A third party should not just be mentioned, but linked to a description of the particular benefits and need satisfactions that they obtained.

The service industry example that follows shows the correct linked use of the benefits (B) and features (F).

Simple statement B–F

For example, 'You will get more assignments if you use Benefits that match the client's Needs'.

Comparison statement B–F–WA–NE

(WA – Wrong action, NE – Negative effect)
For example, 'You will get more assignments if you use Benefits that match the client's Needs. Vague or unrelated Benefits have a low impact.'

Sandwich statement B–F–WA–NE–F–B

For example, 'You will get more assignments if you use Benefits that match the client's Needs. Vague or unrelated Benefits have a low impact; but by carefully selecting Benefits that have a strong appeal you will get more business and get it sooner.'

Obtaining feedback

To ensure that progress is being made towards the ultimate objective, accurate feedback is necessary all the time. It is then possible to be flexible and readjust as the conversation proceeds. By observation, by waiting and listening to the customer's reply, and by asking for a comment, feedback can be assured, at the same time monitoring questions constantly to be answered. Am I discussing your needs? Is this a problem? Is my proposition attractive, clear and convincing? Have I overlooked anything? Whatever is appropriate to ensure that the customer's needs are being satisfied, keep the customer involved in the discussion and prevent problems developing later on.

Presenting one's case is simple and successful if one follows these basic rules:

- Take one point at a time.
- Tell the client what it means to him in terms of results.
- Show him what it is or means.
- Provide proof where necessary.
- Check progress by obtaining constant feedback.

Obtaining feedback and maintaining a two-way aspect to the conversation (yet maintaining control) is crucial. Some of it is as simple as making sure you listen (again). Pardon? Listen, really listen and use, and be seen to use, the information you are given to tailor your case. Anything else will seem like the 'standard patter'.

So far so good

This stage is clearly crucial. It often constitutes the majority of the sales meeting. It should reinforce all the good initial impressions formed by the prospect in the early stages, particularly:

- professionalism
- customer orientation
- technical competence and clear expression

and, generally, an acceptance that 'this is the sort of person we can do business with'.

This is also the stage where real differentiation develops and can become significant, where the prospect begins to log areas where you are different, and more to his liking than the others. This is also where the detail begins to mount up.

While this will not outweigh a poor product or service, it will augment a good one and will contribute to the creation of the right balance as the prospect weighs up what he is being offered.

Session 5

Handling objections

> HANDLING OBJECTIONS
>
> I am important.
> Consider my needs.
> What are the facts?
>
> (What are the snags?)
>
> What shall I do?
> I approve.

Explain that as we all know in sales situations, objections can be barriers.

Salespeople should try to prevent objections arising in the first place by:

1 Making sure that the customer's needs are sufficiently explored
2 Solutions are not offered too soon
3 Not making benefits and features too general. However some will occur
   and are a natural part of the buying process (weighing up).

Write the heading 'OBJECTIONS' on the flip chart

Explain that objections have both an emotional and a rational content:

● emotionally, the customer can become defensive or even aggressive
  write 'Emotional' as a sub-heading

- rationally, he needs a logical answer **write** 'Rational' as a second sub-heading.

These two elements to an objection have to be tackled separately and sequentially.

Techniques for handling objections

Explain that in order to keep emotions under control the first response should be to:

1 Listen.
2 Pause and think.
3 Acknowledge his remarks.

Apparent (or real!) **consideration** of the objection builds the customer's confidence in how it is being dealt with; a rapid, 'glib' response may arouse suspicions.

Note: that it is amazing how much can usefully go through your mind as you pause and say 'That's an important point, Mr. Customer, let's see what we can do to sort it' – the technique buys **time to think**.

In order to provide **rational** answers:

1 Try turning the objection into a question.
2 Establish the customer's need behind his objection and find out **WHY** it's being raised.
3 Match your answer to the objection using an appropriate technique.

For example:

Most of the objections you will face will fall into one of eight categories:

Introduce the first category:

1 **Price objection**: 'It's too expensive'

Problem: The customer believes the financial cost out weighs the value.

Solution: Establish what he means by 'value'

● Emphasise the benefits of the proposal and put a financial value on them

● Get the customer to examine the total costs involved not just the purchase cost

If in your organisation your proposal is likely to be more expensive than competition, then:

Ask the group how they would respond to the customer.

Some typical responses may include:

A Find out if the objection to cost is influenced by any other factors: e.g.

● it's outside the cost authority of the customer
● it's higher than the budget allows
● it's much more than the customer expected
● _____
● _____
● _____

B Explain why it is more expensive in terms of the compensating benefits. In your terms this could be due to:

● higher quality
● reliability
● speeds of service
● _____
● _____
● _____

Make a note of any specific ones you want to mention:

_____

_____

_____

_____

_____

> Price objections are more important than almost any other.
>
> You may want to spend more time analysing what people really mean when they say something like 'It's very expensive'. We cannot, after all, answer until this is known. You may find as many as 20/30 (or more!) ranging from 'I want to negotiate' to 'I have a better quote from someone else' (in which case – for the same thing, or something a little different?). Others include: 'It is more than I expected', 'It is more than last year', 'I am not convinced it is value for money', 'I can't approve that' (someone else perhaps can) – all may need a different response. Never answer an objection without being clear what is meant by it.

2 Fear objection:

The customer believes the proposition has an **unacceptable** disadvantage.

The salesperson has to prove that this fear is understandable but groundless.

Ask the group to think of an example which in your company's proposition would appear to be unacceptable to a customer.

Write this objection on the flip chart.

Ask the group to think of some solutions (give a moment for thought).

List the solutions on the flip chart.

Make a note of any particular points you want to add here:

_____

_____

_____

_____

Emphasise and deal with the range of objections that may need handling, going through the other six main types of objection and **discuss** them with the group in the context of the sort of situation your salesperson might find himself.

The other six are:

3 Habit objection:

'We've always done it this way and we see no reason to change.'

4 Wrong information objection:

'I'm told that your design people are inexperienced in this field.'

5 Detail objection:

'It will mean changing our desktop publishing computer system.'

6 Complaint:

'Your people completely ignored our last delivery instructions.'

7 Competition objection:

'We prefer to use the system our other supplier uses.'

8 Interested party objection:

'I can't give you an answer without consulting with my colleagues.'

Tell the group that you are now going to take on the role of a typical customer and that you will raise objections with individuals in the group. Each individual will have to respond out loud in the way they would in a typical sales meeting situation.

Ask the group to consider a number of objections prepared beforehand.

_____

_____

_____

_____

Examples (following the print example referred to before):

● These print prices are far too high.

● We've tried four-colour printing before, but it did not turn out as well as we expected.

● I can't see any reason to change from our regular printer.

● Our customers will see it as glossy, expensive and reckon it affects our prices to them.

Wait until the response has been fully – and satisfactorily – given before moving on.

Emphasise that you are seeking approaches and a way of thinking about objections, rather than scripted answers.

Discuss briefly the responses given.

Summary

Conclude this section by saying that successful salespeople handle objections by:

1 Keeping the emotional atmosphere under control.
2 Identifying the real needs behind the objections.
3 Using the appropriate answering technique.

Ask for any further questions from the group before proceeding.

TIME:

BACKGROUND NOTES

Handling objections

This stage is less neat. Objections can occur throughout the whole process, though perhaps most come towards the end of the presentational stage. Some objections are inevitable, a part of the weighing-up process buyers go through in which they search for the plus and the minus points of any proposition put to them. In this sense objections can be a sign of interest.

But there are other more down-to-earth reasons why objections arise that are within a salesperson's control:

- He may not have identified and agreed the customer's needs.
- He may have offered his solutions too soon.
- He may have talked features instead of benefits.
- His benefits may have been too general or too numerous.
- He may have failed to obtain or recognise feedback.

Thus, it has to be said that many objections are not inherent in customers; they are caused by salespeople. You should reduce the frequency and intensity of objections by selling well, but from time to time they will still arise.

How to keep control

So, when they do occur, the first thing to recognise is that most objections have both an emotional and rational content. Emotionally, the customer becomes defensive or aggressive! Rationally, he requires a logical answer to the particular objection that he has raised. To handle them successfully you will need to tackle the emotional and rational aspects separately and sequentially.

We will look first at how to handle the emotional aspect and keep things under control. Its importance can be illustrated by the frequency with which current affairs programmes on radio and TV degenerate into slanging matches. If you watch them closely you will see that the trouble starts when one participant says something with which another disagrees. Instead of controlling their emotions and dealing with the point clearly and logically, they criticise each other. The rest you know only too well.

Keeping control is easy if we put ourselves in the customer's position when he finds disadvantages in a proposition. If we were customers, we would want the salesperson to listen to our point of view, to consider it, and to acknowledge that our point was reasonable – and to do so before he answered. We can do the same with objections raised by customers, keep control, and as a result allow him to consider the answer calmly and rationally.

The conversation might go like this. The customer identifies a 'snag' and voices his objections: 'I think the system will be too complicated for our people and, therefore, they won't use it.',

The salesperson listens; pauses; and acknowledges, 'It probably does look complicated to anyone who hasn't seen it before, and we obviously need to take that into account when it's being installed.'

Notice that the salesperson has not yet answered the objection. All he has done is shown understanding of the customer's point of view and met the first point in the buying sequence: 'I am important and want to be respected.'

So often, rational answers to objections are less than successful because the customer is emotionally unable to evaluate them fairly.

By listening, pausing and acknowledging, we keep the customer's emotions under control and give our answers the best chance of being accepted.

Such holding remarks, as in the example just given, may be quite brief – 'That's a good point', 'We will certainly need to consider that' – but, despite this, they may serve another purpose. Human design is such that in the time it takes us to say a phrase, such as 'We will certainly need to consider that', there can be a considerable amount of thinking going on. Such remarks give us a chance so consider what we ought to say next. They can be invaluable if the objection has really thrown you (never let it show on your face or in your manner, incidentally).

Before considering how to answer objections, we must point out that you need to understand what the objection means. Never be afraid to answer a question with a question. Alternatively, if the objection comes as a challenge (without a question mark at the end), it may help to turn the objection into a question, and so establish the customer's need behind his resistance. Why is he asking this? Is it an excuse? Delaying tactics? Perhaps he has a point? An apparently straightforward comment, such as 'It is very expensive', may mean a wide range of different things from 'It is more than I expected' to 'No', from 'It is more than I can agree' (though someone else might) to 'It is very expensive' and so on. For example, on a recent course, participants I asked to think about alternative meanings for the phrase 'It is very expensive' produced 36 within 10 minutes or so, most necessitating a different answer from each other.

Checking the status of the objection does not mean that we do not have to answer it. We do. Think of objections as minus signs, of different sizes, sitting on the balance the customer is conjuring up in his mind. There are only three ways of dealing with them. Either you explain that the point is not valid, and the balance is therefore more positive, as the point is removed from the minus side; or you persuade him it is less significant than he fears, so most of its weight goes; or you agree (there is no merit in trying to convince him black is white). In all three cases, particularly the latter, the sales person's response may need to include some re-emphasis on the positive side also.

You have to know your product/service well to produce a good answer. The following approaches will help.

The boomerang

This approach pushes the question back to the customer:

C 'I am sure I could get something cheaper.'
S 'There are plenty of models around that are less expensive, it's true. However, you were saying earlier that the minimum level of production rejects cannot be exceeded, and the model we are discussing . . .'

Pre-empting

Here the objection is assumed, avoided and dealt with.

S 'You may well feel this only applies to organisations larger than yours, I would like to show you, however, how it has particular benefits for your kind of firm . . .'

Delay

This is as close as you can get to not answering. In fact, you answer later.

C 'Now, before we get into the detail, I am concerned about the level of training this machine necessitates. Just how long is involved?'

S 'That's crucial, of course, I am sure your staff have enough to do already, but it does depend on which model suits you best. Perhaps we can explore that and come back to training.'

Tacit denial

This leaves the point on one side, and concentrates on balancing factors.

C 'The capital cost is too high.'
S 'Well, it isn't the cheapest solution, but the maintenance costs will be less than now and the quality achieved higher.'

Final objections

Here, whatever the query, it is investigated thus.

S 'Apart from delivery, is there anything else you need to be satisfied about before placing an order?'

The customer can then say that everything else is fine, or produce a list to be dealt with. The former remark is particularly useful near to the end of the meeting as a lead into the close.

There is a need to deal promptly and definitely (not glibly) with objections; you have to have the courage of your convictions and sometimes a simple, but sound, answer to seemingly dramatic objections that meets the point head on changes the flow of the conversation. A price objection, 'That's very expensive', met simply with, 'Yes, it is a considerable investment', may be followed by a long pause, after which the prospect moves on to something else.

As a final illustration, we will stay with price objections. Any mechanism which prompts the right response, to any objection in fact, is useful. With price, the following, using the mathematical symbols as a prompt to memory, leads into some good responses:

Sign	The words you should use to emphasise what the price will mean
+ (benefits)	add; added-value; in addition; plus; augment; reinforce; enhance; strengthen; develop.
– (losses)	less; reduce; minimise; contraction; condense; restrict; exclude.
× (productivity)	multiply; considerable; numerous; ample; productivity; performance; majority.
÷ (product cost)	share; divide; proportion; amortise; part; distribute; measure.
= (totally of package)	equal; equivalent; will mean; will produce; total; ultimately; outcome; benefit; results.

Handling Objections

- anticipate likely objections
- select and deal with appropriate ones before they are raised
- be seen to respond in a considered manner
- do not be – or at least appear to be – caught out

You should rarely be caught out by objections you have not foreseen, at least in general terms. Thus, handling them effectively is another result of good preparation. There will always be some, however, that demand you are 'quick on your feet'. An apparently unexpected objection, well-handled, can be impressive, and taken as a display of competence.

Use prevention and cure to handle objections effectively.

Objections have to be dealt with; but, remember, although 'What are the snags?' is an instinctive part of the buying process, by the time the customer reaches this stage he may be sufficiently attracted by the proposal to pass on without raising objections. It pays to concentrate on resistance prevention rather than resistance cure. Agreement on stated needs, and careful selection and presentation of need-related benefits, reduces both the frequency and strength of resistance.

So far so good

While you do not want to encourage objections, quite the reverse, in fact, objection handling is as much prevention as cure, and you can gain from them.

This occurs primarily in two ways. First, objections provide information, and the better the information available in total, the easier it is to sell. The first information they give is that there is interest, since prospects will not bother with any objections if there is no interest. They also provide information about the focus of interest. What concerns the buyer most? What does he, or does he not, understand? And so on.

Secondly, good objection handling is a display of professional competence and can raise your stock with the buyer. Indeed, some objections are voiced specifically as a test ('Let's see how they handle this!').

So, the professional sales person minimises objections, but handles the inevitable ones well, professionally, in a way that builds up the image of him and his product or service. A glib answer, evasion, argument or a stunned silence will all lose credibility which, at this stage, should be building up positively and well.

Session 6

Closing

CLOSING

I am important.
Consider my needs.
What are the facts?
What are the snags?

What shall I do?

I approve.

Emphasise again that the main objective in the selling process is to obtain customer commitment.

Attempts to obtain a commitment (close) without first having created a desire for our proposition will normally be seen by the buyer as pressure tactics.

Closing does not cause orders. It prompts action converting high desire into orders and low desire into refusals.

Even when desire is high, the customer may not volunteer a positive commitment. Similarly, the customer may want to make a commitment, but there are several variations of it, he wants one particular kind.

Emphasise that it is in these situations that effective closing skills are invaluable.

Recognising buying signals

Introduce this section by explaining that there are certain types of behaviour, question and comments that can indicate the buyer's willingness to buy.

Some of these include:

Tone of voice, posture, hesitation, nodding

Questions on details showing acceptance in principle

Comments expressing positive interest attraction etc.

 Ask the group for examples they have come across in spotting a buyer's willingness to buy.

Illustrate the variety of approaches to closing. Examples of each method are given below with space for your own versions.

 Write the name of each method on the flip chart.

Method	*Example*	*Example*
Direct request (just a question)	'Right, do we go ahead?'	_____
Command (tell them)	'Get the confirmation organised and we will start at the beginning of the next month'	_____
Alternatives (the 'yes' or 'yes' (question)	'Do we go ahead with plan A or B'	_____

Immediate gain (money/timing/ people)	'If you can give me the go ahead now, I can guarantee completion by the end of the month' (and John will head up the project team) _____
Assumption (proceeding as if they had said 'yes')	'Fine, what I suggest we do now is … and we will deliver at the end of the month' _____
Best solution (or summary)	'So, to get things complete by the end of the month, do the job cost-effectively and without internal hassle we should go ahead now. Right?' _____
Final objection (following a 'No')	'You're saying no because you are still not convinced we can make the deadline?' 'Yes' 'If I can persuade you we can, will you go ahead?' 'Yes, I suppose we would.' 'Right, let's see how we can ensure meeting that deadline …' _____

The examples can come from you or from the group.

Ask the group to write down closing statements suitable as responses to a series of four customer comments in the form of a close; you can suggest these comments or ask for suggestions.

Examples on such comments might be phrases like:

- How soon can you deliver?
- This looks impressive.
- I like the quality.
- This matches our requirement well.
- How are these normally supplied?

Make a note of some suitable phrases from your business that will be appropriate:

_____

_____

_____

_____

_____

Allow about 5–10 minutes for this to be done.

Now **ask** for feedback on the exercise, going through each comment in turn.

Then discuss briefly.

Summarise

Emphasise again the importance of closing and how all the other stages lead up to this.

Ask for any further questions from the group before proceeding.

TIME:

At this point you will have reviewed the complete sequential process of the face-to-face sales situation.

Emphasise that selling is a dynamic process, and that it not only improves the practice, but the techniques have to be deployed customer by customer, meeting by meeting. It is the precision of this deployment that makes for success.

Explain that an integral part of the course is role-play – an opportunity to practice – to experiment – in the safety of our own group and as a basis for extending the discussion of the process with the examples role-playing will create.

The next section sets, out the procedure (more detailed background on role-playing technique is given on page 169).

BACKGROUND NOTES

Closing

Closing is not really a stage. It is a question and a prompt to customer commitment and action. The first rule about closing is simple. Do it! It is all too easy for closing to be avoided, and with it, of course, the trauma of 'Will he say "no"?'. But a close that is no more than, say, 'Does that tell you all you need at the moment? – getting a pleasant response like 'Yes, thank you so much for all your help', followed by 'Goodbye' – is not really worthy of the term 'close'.

Note, however, that closing does not only apply to getting the order. We want commitments at many stages, especially in complex sales situations. The prospect may agree to:

- a meeting
- a demonstration
- receive samples/literature
- attend an exhibition
- another meeting (or formal presentation)
- a written proposal or quotation.

All these, and more – sometimes in a sequence – are steps on the way to the sale and need the commitment gained just as much as with the order at the end of the day.

Obtaining commitment

Knowing that the objective of all selling is to obtain customer commitments often obscures the need to remember how buyers arrive at the point of commitment. They only willingly take buying decisions after they have recognised and felt needs, and are convinced that their needs will be satisfied by implementing the proposal. Thus, the best chance of success lies in doing a good job before they reach the stage of asking themselves 'What shall I do?'.

Attempts to get commitment (closing) without first having created desire for the proposition will normally be seen by the customer as pressure tactics. The bigger the decision, the greater the pressure, and the stronger will be the resistance.

Closing does not cause orders, it merely converts a high desire into orders and low desire into refusals. Even when the desire is high, however, the customer may not volunteer a positive commitment. Similarly, the customer may want to make a commitment, but there are several variations of it, and the salesperson wants one particular kind. It is in these situations that closing skills are valuable; such skills concentrate the buyer's mind on the advantages to be gained from the buying decision itself.

There are certain behaviours, questions and comments indicating a general willingness to buy that can provide 'buying signals', indicating the best moment at which to close. Tone of voice, posture, hesitation, nodding, questions on details, showing acceptance in principle, or comments expressing positive interest are all examples. These can be converted into closes, as long as you are careful not to oversell when the customer wants to make a commitment.

So, whether closing is successful or not is dependent on two things. First, there is everything you have done to date. If the preceding stages have not succeeded in stimulating sufficient interest, or if there are still objections niggling at the interest, then there is little likelihood of closing securing final agreement.

Secondly, the closing question must be put in an appropriate and positive fashion. Thus, although this is the crunch point and can sometimes be avoided because of the unpleasant possibility of getting a 'No', the commitment must actually be asked for; the only question is exactly how it is put. There are various methods. Here are some examples.

Direct request

For example, 'Shall we go ahead then and start getting these improvements in service levels?'

Requests like this should be used where the customer likes to make his own decisions.

Command

For example, 'Install this new system in each regional office. It will give you the information you want much more quickly and help you to make more effective decisions.'

This can be used where the customer:

- has difficulty in making a decision or
- has considerable respect for the salesperson.

Immediate gain

For example, 'You mentioned that this year the company really needs to improve productivity. If you can give me the go-ahead now, I can make sure that you see specific results within three months' time.'

This could be used where, by acting fast, the customer can get an important benefit, whereas delay might cause him severe problems. The 'hard' version of this is the . . .

Fear close

As in 'Unless you can give me the go ahead . . .'. This is a more powerfully phrased version of 'immediate gain', and should be used with discretion.

Alternatives

For example, 'Both these approaches meet your criteria. Which one do you prefer to implement?'

This could be used where the salesperson is happy to get a commitment on any one of the possible alternatives.

'Best solution'

For example, 'You want a system that can cope with occasional off-peak demands, that is easy to operate by semi-skilled staff and is presented in a form that will encourage line managers to use it. The best fit with all these requirements is our system "X" When's the best time to install it?'

This should be used when the customer has a mix of needs some of which can be better met by the competition, but which, when taken as a whole, are best met by your solution.

Question or objection

For example, 'If we can make that revision, can you get the finance director to agree to proceed?'

This should be used where you know you can answer the customer's objection to his satisfaction.

Assumption

For example, 'Fine. I've got all the information I need to meet your requirements. As soon as I get back to the office I'll prepare the necessary paperwork and you'll have delivery by the end of next week.'

In other words, we assume the customer has said 'Yes' and continue the conversation on this basis.

Concession

Trade only a small concession to get agreement now or agree to proceed only on stage one.

So far so good, our closing question is slipped in as a natural part of the conversation. It should provide the customer with an appropriate moment at which to confirm his willingness to act. The answer at this point may well be 'Yes'.

No matter how well a presentation is given and questions handled in selling, the prospect may still sometimes have objections to making a decision. Sometimes these are stated, but often they are reserved and come in the form, 'I'll think about it'.

When this happens, simple closes may only irritate the prospect and the way forward may be unclear. Yet it is a key stage to get over, and this can be done by listing the objections, 'I agree you should think about it. However, it's possibly your experience also that when someone says they want to think about it it's because they are still uncertain about some points. In order to help our thinking on these, let's note them down.' Then make a list with room for more objections than he has; do not write any down until each is understood, and do not answer any – yet. Flush them all out and be sure there are not more to come. This enables an additional closing technique to be used, 'If I'm able to answer each of these points to your complete satisfaction, can we agree we're in business?'. This is the *conditional close*. Each point listed is answered in turn, crossed off the list, and the prospect's agreement with each checked, then the close is not repeated, but assumption used to conclude matters, 'Fine, now we're in business'.

Having made a commitment, a customer may need reassurance that he has done the right thing. Always thank him, confirm that he has made a wise decision, touch once more on what will come from it, conclude and leave promptly. If you hang about, the customer may start to rethink matters and the good that has been done may start to be undone! When the customer has been satisfied on the first points in the buying process, a close, emphasising the need satisfaction that a commitment will bring, will naturally convert desire into action. Good selling can often make formal closing unnecessary, 'Make him thirsty and you won't have to force him to drink'.

Of course, the commitment given may not be to do business. The necessity for 'steps on the way' has been referred to previously, when setting objectives was reviewed.

In many businesses, if you cannot close, you cannot sell. It is crucial. It must be done positively and in a way that positions it as the natural conclusion to satisfactory discussions.

Further, closing sets the scene for a good future relationship; if you help people to buy something with which they are subsequently satisfied, they will come back for more. Today's satisfied customers are tomorrow's best prospects. The salesperson himself is an important part of any decision by the buyer 'to repeat the experience, or discuss larger requirements for the future.

Regard closing as a beginning, and you will do better in future.

Closing

- recognise that everything you do leads up to closing
- watch for 'buying signals'
- close at the right moment
- match closing technique to individual customers

Some of the available business will go to those prepared to tie it down positively. It can be awkward actually to say, 'Right, when do we start?', or whatever. This is probably because we know they could say 'No'. But not asking – or saying – 'Please think about it', leaves us open to our more positive thinking competition.

Be positive, watch for, and overcome any psychological fear of closing, and go for it.

Summary

People may buy from people they do not like, nor even respect, if the product is good enough. However, they are more likely to buy if everything done throughout the meeting says that the salesperson is a professional.

So, finally, there are certain factors that tend to be buyers' 'pet hates', that is they have a disproportionately negative impact, especially if a buyer finds a number of them cropping up in one meeting. So, beware, if you do not get to the point quickly enough, or are too abrupt you may be in trouble. Similarly, talking too much and not asking enough questions (or asking them, but ignoring the answers); appearing inadequately informed about the product/service, the market or competition (or giving the impression you know it all)'; interrupting the buyer or ignoring his stated needs or preferences; putting on too much pressure (but equally neglecting to close); displaying a lack of self-confidence (or trying too hard); being scruffy, impolite, whining about the poor market or unfair competition; failing to take an interest in the buyer, his situation or to express any enthusiasm for the whole process; all can create a negative reaction. Any failure to communicate clearly makes things worse.

In all we have reviewed about the face-to-face meeting, individually the elements are really only common sense. There is a good deal to remember, however; a good deal to keep in mind as you actually go through the meeting and attempt to fine-tune what you are doing. And the small details are as important as the overall structure; many a sale must have been won or lost on the inclusion of one extra phrase or more detailed description, or the exclusion of something that dilutes the case. The greatest challenge is perhaps orchestrating the whole process. So, avoid the pitfalls, be particularly aware of those areas of the process that potentially create an edge and your strike rate will be better.

Session 7

The sales meeting role-play

For this exercise to work well you need at least six people in the group, though the overall approach can be easily adapted to other numbers of participants.

You will need to work out the time available for this session from the time it will take each pair to do each section of the role play and the amount of comment and discussion that will be necessary.

Note: the precise way in which role-playing is undertaken with a group can, of course, vary. One particular format is set out here but this can be adapted to suit your objectives, style and the number of participants. You may want to read the section on role play in Section 3 before finally deciding how you will handle this session.

What you will need

1 If you are using video equipment you will need a kit comprising:

- a camera with automatic focusing and exposure (most modern cameras have a setting that works well indoors)
- a tripod for the camera
- a VHS recorder (if not built into the camera) with a counter to identify where you are and allow you to find specific points
- a microphone which can be mounted on a table/desk
- a TV monitor which can present the pictures and sound from the recorder

- spare video tapes
- the necessary cables and leads to connect the equipment.

It is always advisable to carry out a short test recording and playback before the role-play starts to ensure that pictures and sound are recording properly.

2 Role-play briefs – hand these out to the group so that they can refer to them during your instructions.

Room preparation

An example of a practical layout is suggested, though room restrictions may, of course, dictate otherwise (see Chart on page 176)

Role-play briefs

The intention is that the role-play takes place around real customer situations, indeed it can even be a rehearsal for a real meeting.

You need, therefore, to select and write up the key essentials of such a situation.

Examples of the format for role-play briefs for the salesperson and customer follow; these provide the bare outline of what will be necessary.

It may be worth including reference to:

- the nature and size of the customer (i.e. organisation)
- whether it is a first or follow-up meeting
- something about potential
- the position, role and authority of the customer

Make a note of any other factors you wish to include

_____

_____

_____

_____

_____

Such a brief can either be prepared by the leader or, time permitting, by those playing the sales role selecting a situation and briefing the buyer. The latter can be carried out before or during the session.

Once the role-play is under way both parties should add details as necessary, and the scenario will develop as it is enacted.

SALESMAN'S ROLE-PLAY BRIEF

Objective: to secure an order, after completing the sales meeting.

The interview is between yourself and
Mr _____ , the senior buyer
with _____ Ltd

You have made an appointment with Mr _____ . He is expecting you and, although he knows of your company, he knows very little of the detail of what you offer.

The role-play opens with you knocking on Mr _____ 's door.

CUSTOMER'S ROLE-PLAY BRIEF

You are Mr _____ . You are the senior buyer with _____ Ltd. The company's key operations include _____ .

Your company's current needs/problems are _____ _____ .
Your overall budget is £ _____ . If possible you would like to have the solution to your need/problem solved, supplied and delivered within the next _____ weeks.

You have invited a number of potential suppliers to see you.

The role-play opens with the salesperson knocking on your door. You are expecting him and, although you know of the company you know very little about their services as yet.

You may wish to produce a tailored version of each format.

How to organise the role-play

1 **Explain** to the group that the sales interview is going to be divided into three stages:

The opening

The main presentation

Objections and the close

(other arrangements are of course possible)

2 **Divide** the group into pairs and explain that each pair will be asked to role-play one of the stages of the sales interview. One person will be the salesperson and the other the customer.

3 **Hand out** the role-play briefs with each pair deciding which role they wish to play. You will need to work out the details and situation of the customer and his company and either fill in the briefs or let the participants fill them in to your instructions.

4 **Explain** how the role play will be conducted.

Say that the main objective is to reinforce skill in managing and controlling a sales interview

Emphasise that the exercise should be regarded as an opportunity to experiment and that it does not matter if mistakes are made in individual performances – it is more important to improve 'awareness' of how a good sales meeting is conducted so that improvements can be made in the future

Explain that the first pair will do the first stage – 'the opening'. They will be stopped at an appropriate point and the second pair will continue with stage two of the interview – 'the main presentation' – without losing the flow of the conversation and building upon what has already been established. Again this will be stopped at an appropriate point and a pair will be invited to continue the same interview with Stage 3 – 'Objections/close' – building again upon the facts and agreements already established.

As an option you could **assign** one member of the group to be camera operator. They could also stop and start the video cassette recorder. You could, of course, do this yourself if you prefer.

Explain that you will be recording the numbers on the video cassette recorder number counter for the start, finish and points of interest of each interview so that you can identify which sequences to play back later.

Give any instructions you think necessary for operating the equipment.

Camera operators can be changed for each series of interviews so that everyone is involved.

Ask the group for any questions they may have

5 Now **start** the first role-play

Ask the participants to take their seats and ask if they have any questions. Answer them ensuring that they know what they have to do.

Note: it is really very important that everyone is clear **exactly** how this session will work. You may wish to circulate written guidelines at an appropriate stage. The background note sets out an example .

BACKGROUND NOTES

Example: written role-play instruction

The sales meeting role-play

1 The main objective of this exercise is to reinforce skills in managing and controlling a sales interview. It should be regarded as an opportunity to experiment so that new techniques can be tried out before being applied in a real customer situation.

2 In this exercise a typical sales meeting is broken down into three key stages:

- the opening
- the main presentation
- objections/the close.

3 The course leader will divide the group into pairs and each pair will role-play one of these stages. One person will role-play the sales person and the other the customer.

4 You will either be asked to select a customer situation or be supplied with a brief about one. Thus both sales person and customer have basic information as a starting point and can add to this as the session progresses.

You should consider what company support material (e.g. literature/visual aids/samples) you think would be needed at the kind of meeting involved, using this as appropriate.

5 The first pair will role-play the first stage and at an appropriate point will be stopped and the second pair will be invited to pick up

and continue the conversation with the second stage. This should be a continuation of the first stage without losing its direction and building upon what has already been established.

Again at an appropriate point this role-play will be stopped and a third pair will be invited to continue with the same sales conversation, also without losing direction and building upon the facts and agreements already established.

6 Throughout the interview you (as salesperson or customer) may introduce new information. However, if you do, this must:

- not be designed to 'catch out' either the salesperson or customer unreasonably.
- not directly contradict whatever has already been established and agreed
- sensibly reflect real-life situations.

7 The role-plays will continue until a clear conclusion has been reached or the allotted time has expired.

8 You will be given an opportunity to view and comment upon the video recordings.

This is an opportunity not only to 'critique' how individual inputs have gone, but to discuss typical factors likely to repeat in other meetings for any of the group, how a particular explanation can be made clearly, how an objection might be tackled and so on.

Give the instruction to start recording (checking that there is a video cassette in the recorder and that you have recorded the initial counter tape numbers) then:

Ask for the first interview to start.

Make sure that you are seated so that you can see the interview and the video cassette number counter clearly As well as recording the start and finish of each interview **record the position of useful learning points as the conversation proceeds to facilitate playback later.**

Stop the interview at an appropriate point and pause the video recorder in the record mode if possible. If this is not possible stop the recorder recording. Check that the counter numbers and names of participants are recorded.

Ask the second pair to take up their places and start recording again. Check that counter numbers and names of participants are recorded.

Repeat for the third pair and check that the counter numbers are recorded.

Ask for initial impressions from those who were salespeople, customers and from the group.

Continue with the above sequence if you have more than six in the group

Now play back the first stage of the (first) interview. Stopping the tape at suitable learning points and initiating discussion from the group. Remember that you should be trying to build on strengths, as well as trying to highlight weaknesses, and demonstrate better ways of working.

The **checklist** suggests some practical guidelines regarding exactly how to critique the role-play examples.

Continue this procedure through all the interviews. If time is running short it may be necessary to 'fast forward' through some parts of the interviews.

Ask for any final comments or observations and thank and praise all the participants for their contributions .

TIME:

CHECKLIST:
GETTING THE MOST FROM ROLE-PLAY

To recap: role-play is useful in two distinct ways:

- in providing immediate feedback about individual performance

- in producing common examples of the kind of interaction that all salespeople must be able to handle (and showing something about how they can be successfully handled as well as, on other occasions, how they should not be tackled).

While there is a case for saying that selling is based on common sense, certainly in terms of its individual techniques, it is also a complex and dynamic social skill. In other words there is a great deal going on in a typical sales interview.

What lessons and discussion opportunities the role-play enactments produce should not be left entirely to chance, nor should you attempt to comment on every aspect of every session or the whole process quickly becomes unmanageable. You need a planned approach to the analysis.

First, bear in mind that there are two kinds of activity which deserve comment and debate:

1 **Isolated technique** – how someone opens, how they handle an individual objection or close; and all other factors that occur at particular moments in the interview.

2 **Overall factors** – clarity of explanation, focus on the customer and other factors which should be strong throughout the interview.

Playback and discussion will usefully focus on both.

It is worth designing for yourself a checklist of the points you want to cover in discussion. You may want to be comprehensive, or focus on topical areas or current weaknesses: how best to describe a new product or overcome a new and troublesome objection, perhaps.

Separate the two kinds of factor:

Isolated factors	*Overall factors*
E.g. Opening remarks	E.g. Clarify of description
Benefit description of an individual product	Empathy to customer needs

_____ _____

_____ _____

_____ _____

_____ _____

_____ _____

_____ _____

_____ _____

_____ _____

_____ _____

_____ _____

_____ _____

Then decide which elements to principally examine after each individual role-play. On the one hand you can make, or allow, some general comments about each, on the other you may want to suggest a focus: 'Let's look particularly at the main presentation in this one.' If you do this in a different way across a number of role-plays you will maintain a greater variety and can still plan to cover your complete list of chosen topics by the time you reach the last role-play example.

In this way you will make sure you conduct a lively session and that the most is learned from it. Two final points:

- Balance the time spent on individual comments and the more general issues raised (the latter should probably take the majority of the time).
- Balance the good and the bad – the session must not become an acrimonious witch hunt – and it is often good practice to start and finish with the good.

A session such as this can be a powerful force for circulating good ideas. Often one member of a team has worked out a good way of dealing with some aspect of meetings with which others still have some trouble. Such an idea – as it is or adapted – may be just what others are looking for to help. Remember to give credit. Note it as so-and-so's idea – better still, if the overall output of role-play analysis is what *we* have worked out between us (rather than simply what people have been told) it will be that much more useful and the lessons will be that much more likely to stick.

VIDEO TAPE NUMBER RECORD FORM

TAPE NUMBERS		ACTIONS/WORDS	
From	To	Salesman	Customer
_____	_____	_____	_____
_____	_____	_____	_____
_____	_____	_____	_____
_____	_____	_____	_____
_____	_____	_____	_____
_____	_____	_____	_____
_____	_____	_____	_____
_____	_____	_____	_____
_____	_____	_____	_____
_____	_____	_____	_____
_____	_____	_____	_____
_____	_____	_____	_____
_____	_____	_____	_____
_____	_____	_____	_____

Session 8

....

Main Course Summary

When role-playing is complete:

Review briefly the main parts of the course:

Call planning

The sales interview

- opening a call
- the main presentation
- handling objections
- closing the sale

The role play

Write on the flip chart and ask the group for feedback on the key lessons of the course and how they may change the way they do things in future. It may help if you prompt feedback by focusing selectively on key sections of the course. (You can always note others to return to later – at a subsequent sales meeting, for instance.)

List some of the key points made, and **ask participants** to make notes on action they will be taking.

Ask for any further questions or comments and then thank all the participants for their contributions **and draw the course to a close with an enthusiastic and forward-looking final word** – end on a high note (never with the ubiquitous 'Any other business').

TIME:

3

....

TRAINING TECHNIQUES

Any training is dependent for its success on a number of factors. These include how well it relates to identified needs, how relevant it is to the real day-to-day job of participants, how participative it is, and more. The previous section, running chronologically through the workshop, was self-contained. Given both time to go through this and some, albeit small, degree of tailoring then the workshop that can be run from it can meet many of the criteria for successful and effective training. But one other factor is key: that is the way in which it is put over. The effectiveness of training messages, like humour, is dependent on 'the way you tell'em'.

This section is not intended to be a complete run-down on training techniques, indeed your experience may well mean that you do not need this in any case. Rather it is designed to highlight key issues, as either an introduction or to recap, and provide within this overall volume comment on everything that is necessary to run the session. It is arranged in four sections:

- presentational techniques
- techniques to prompt and handle participation
- the methodology of role-playing, which as has been said in the previous section can be of valuable assistance in developing sales skills
- the use of training films

which are now dealt with in turn.

Presentational techniques

Whoever is putting across the workshop, how it is received will be dependent in part on the way it is presented. So presentation is important. But there is more to it than simply putting on a performance that is stimulating and sends people away with a warm glow as it were; you are seeking to ensure learning takes place and that practice, and thus results, change as a consequence. So the detail of how things are done is also important.

This section is designed to highlight key factors which can be used to make your presentation more effective. If you see what you are to do as helping people to learn, in any case an excellent definition of training, then it makes sense to start this review with the group in mind and consider what helps people to learn.

Ensuring learning takes place

There are several classic ways of positively assisting this process:

- **Making the message relevant**. You need to keep the nature of the group in mind throughout, to make sure that what is said is in their language, relates to the real job they have to do and fits into their frame of reference. If the group see the training message as tailored to them, representing their situation and if, above all, they think it will help them do the job better or more easily – or both – then they will take an interest and learn. Having clear, stated objectives for the session and seeking participants' agreement to them is also important.

- **Use a logical order**. Any message is going to be easier to take on board if it is not a struggle to work out, so creating a good, clear and logical path through the content is important. The workshop material gives the material here a clear structure, and the working method ensures that logic comes over to delegates.

- **Use appropriate emphasis**. The message must prompt a concentration on it. This is helped by a number of things, such as varying the pace, but also by repetition. Never be afraid to repeat, albeit in a different way, the key elements of the content. It is the combination of methods – lecture, discussion, an exercise etc. – that can do this and really enhance the likelihood of participants retaining the essentials of the message.

With this in mind we can turn more directly to how to make the presentation work.

Do not assume it is easy

Any kind of communication can be, perhaps surprisingly, difficult. The difficulties stem from various factors, which, taking a positive view, means you must:

- vary the pace and keep up the interest as peoples' natural tendency is to let their minds wander rather than concentrate continuously

- work at achieving understanding by avoiding too much unfamiliar jargon, using visual aids to reinforce points, choosing your words carefully and fighting peoples' instinct to make judgments too soon by anticipating – often inaccurately – the totality of the message before it is even complete

- accept change is always seen as threatening until its usefulness is clear; if you advocate change make sure you explain both how it can be achieved and what good results will flow from it – for the members of the group

- accept also that there will be plenty of preconceived views and existing memories that act as filters to what you are saying; these may have to be aired and disposed of along the way if a new way is be replace them

- use feedback; the good presenter, and the good trainer, never stops for a second taking in how the group feels (formally by, for example, asking questions and informally by such methods as observation of expressions and reactions), and uses the information gleaned in this way to fine-tune their approach as they go along.

All these points speak of care being necessary and also flexibility.

Preparation

The difficulties mentioned above dictate the three key rules for successful presentation: prepare, prepare and prepare. It is that important. This does not necessarily imply a lengthy process – certainly the workshop set out in this book is specifically in a form that is designed to minimise preparation time – but whatever is done must be done thoroughly and systematically. There is no substitute for being truly familiar with the material in front of you, it will not only facilitate progress through the material but make you more confident and thus more able to fine-tune, respond to questions and digress where appropriate and useful. A key part of preparation is creating guidelines that you can keep in front of you and which act as an effective prompt and make it easy to work through the content; the workshop material does just that and allows you to personalise as necessary.

The group

It may seem obvious but the session is not yours, it is the group's and all the focus of its preparation and delivery must reflect that. Ask yourself how it will be seen, does it reflect their needs, can it be used in their jobs – any question that will enhance this focus. The presenter who prepares only to make it easier for themselves is not so likely to create a session that will work well for others.

A second point here is important and concerns how the group will see you. Any lesson is more likely to be taken on board coming from someone the group respect rather than from someone perceived as trying to 'teach their grandmother to suck eggs'. A well-prepared presentation, even a well-turned out presenter, makes a difference. Your knowledge and your professionalism can enhance learning. On the one hand you need to be perceived as the 'expert', at least to some degree; on the other hand you should talk about the 'opportunities *we* have to improve sales performance', rather than saying something that comes over as 'you people must get your act together'. As was stated earlier training is helping people to learn.

The third point is to bear in mind that training is often perceived as a cure for weak performance. In order to create an atmosphere where training is welcomed by the group it is vital to ensure that the event is seen other than as criticism. Stating that you intend to build on strengths, listing successes, talking about *even better results*, all help this process. The need for sales training is often linked to external change. This may range from increased competition to new customer expectations. Whatever the situation, even if there *are* some weaknesses of performance, you must start the exercise in a way that will make it more likely that people will listen and participate with an open mind.

Structure

After preparation, the greatest asset to good presentation is a sound structure. The workshop material has this built in, but the principles are worth reviewing and are gone through now in a way that takes in some of the other presentational 'tricks of the trade'.

The oldest maxim about communications is also one that offers good advice here: 'Tell'em, tell'em and tell'em'. This means you should tell people what you are going to tell them (introduction), tell them (the main content) and then tell them what you have told them (summary). Whatever else you aim to do this one thought will act to keep you on track. However, it is not sufficient to have a structure, you must make sure it is visible and develop it as you go along, a process sometimes referred to as 'Signposting'. Frankly it is hardly possible to indulge in too much signposting as a session proceeds; it is a technique which allows the group to keep everything you say in context. They know the objectives, they know the structure and where you are in the sequence, how it fits in with what has been covered to date and what will come later, and can follow the thread that much more easily than with less information of this sort.

So, the overall structure is the classic: a beginning, a middle and an end. And each of these may have the same, thus the four main segments of the workshop which reflect the classic stages of the sale all need an internal structure. Consider the three in turn.

The beginning

It is a common cliche that you only get one chance to make a good first impression; but it is true. It is always right to get off to a good start. People make rapid judgments at the start of the session ('Am I going to like this? Will it be useful?'); a good start gets them in the right frame of mind and is also good for the presenter's confidence.

At the beginning of the whole session all the preliminaries need to be dealt with – the welcome, the administration and so on – and, at the same time, you must:

- gain the group's attention
- create (or begin to do so) the necessary rapport.

The first can be helped by a striking start:

- asking a question (even a rhetorical one)
- using a quotation (to make a point in a memorable manner)
- telling a story, an anecdote, or a true, recent or memorable occurance
- stating a striking fact, a statistic say
- using something visual, a slide, a gesture to create impact

or something just downright intriguing to give the necessary impact.

The second is helped by an immediate display of empathy, a focus on the group and how they see things and sheer enthusiasm – always potentially infectious – for the event and the topic.

Using an OHP

Some care should be taken in using overhead projectors to begin with; they appear deceptively simple, but present inherent hazards to the unwary. The following hints may be useful:

- Make sure the electric flex is out of the way (or taped to the floor); ralling over it will improve neither training nor dignity.

- Make sure you have a spare bulb (and know how to change it) – though many machines contain a spare you can switch over to automatically – test both.

- Make sure it is positioned as you want; for example, on a stand or a table on which there is room for notes, etc. Left-handed people will want it placed differently from right-handed people.

- Stand back and to the side of it; it is easy to obscure the view or the screen.

- Having made sure that the picture is in focus, look primarily at thce machine and not at the screen; the machine's prime advantage is to keep you facing the front.

- Only use slides that have big enough typefaces or images and, if you plan to write on acetate, check that the size of your handwriting is appropriate.

- Switch off while changing slides, otherwise the group see a jumbled image as one is removed and replaced by another.

- If you want to project the image on a slide progressively you can cover the bottom part of the image with a sheet of paper (use paper that is not too thick and you will be able to see the image through it, although the covered portion will not project).

- For handwritten use, an acetate roll, rather than sheets, fitted running from the back of the machine to the front will minimise the amount of acetate used (it is expensive!).

- Remember that when something new is shown, all attention goes, at least momentarily, to the slide; as concentration on what you are saying will be less, stop talking until this moment has passed.

- It may be useful to add emphasis by highlighting certain things on slides as you go through them; if you slip the slide *under* a sheet or roll of acetate you can do so without marking the slide.

- Similarly, two slides shown together can add information (this may be done with overlays attached to the slide and folded across); alternatively, the second slide may have minimal information on it, with such things as a course title, session heading or company logo remaining in view through the whole, or part of, the session.

If you want to point something out, this is most easily done by laying a small pointer (or pencil) on the projector. Extending pointers are (in my view) almost impossible to use without looking pretentious, and they risk you having to look over your shoulder.

The middle

This is the core of the session, and must:

- review the content in detail
- ensure acceptance of the message
- maintain the attention of the group.

The structure and 'signposting' referred to above will keep the content unfolding logically and smoothly. Sufficient examples and anecdotes will exemplify what is said, add credibility and make it live; they will also help maintain interest especially if the session is kept reasonably participative with questions and discussion acting as raisins in the bread. Make sure the words you use are sufficiently descriptive, for example you cannot say:

"This is like......" too often. As the details of the core content come through here, the visual aids used will help maintain concentration and concentrate memory (and have an additional advantage as an extra aid to the presenter's memory).

In research carried out on behalf of Kodak, it appears that people take in information in a way that is made up of:

Visual 55 per cent
Tone of voice 37 per cent
Words 8 per cent

Assuming this is correct, it is vital to create visual inputs for as much of the message as possible to increase the chances of more being taken in and remembered. It is because of this that this workshop suggests so much is put up on the flip chart which is the easiest form of visual aid likely to be available. Other methods make visuals – rather than words – easier to handle and the Overhead projector (OHP) is the next most readily available device with this characteristic. So it is perhaps worth a short digression – checklist style – to set out some of the principles of using this ubiquitous but initially somewhat awkward piece of equipment.

The end

Whether of the whole session or just of a segment of it, the final stage is an important one. There is a need to summarise and a need to end on a high note. The end is a pulling together; there should be no loose ends or unanswered questions, and, particularly, participants should leave confident that they have found something useful and, moreover, are well placed to implement what they have reviewed.' The very end may consist of some sort of flourish. A quote, a punchy remark, an injunction to act, a little humour perhaps may all be appropriate on occasions. And the final word will often be a 'thank you', if the group have worked hard, paid attention and you feel action will follow then this is not all your doing, it is theirs too, so thanks are then certainly in order.

Summary (practising what I preach!)

Here the key elements have been touched on, but it is a large topic. Nothing is worse than being on your feet ill prepared and struggling (except perhaps being a member of the group experiencing such a presentation!). Preparation is therefore the key. Preparation lays down the structure and makes the message intelligible, and that structure then helps you smoothly through the whole thing. Such a basis also gives confidence to the presenter. The whole rationale of this publication is to make the whole process of getting a session on sales technique together easier and more certain, but final preparation and implementation is with you and attention to detail pays dividends.

Two final thoughts, then the checklist (in the boxed paragraph) can act as summary: first, timing – stick scrupulously to the timings you work out and particularly make sure participants respect the timings laid down for breaks, exercises and so on. Anything else leads to some degree of chaos.

Secondly, training (unlike some other kinds of presentations) must be participative. This has to be accommodated in parallel into the smooth progress through the session and is the topic of the next section. So read on; if I said it will change your life, I would be finishing this section on a high note (though I might also be exaggerating).

CHECKLIST

Key principles of presentation

Overall have:

- clear objectives
- a sound, and stated, structure
- a focus on the audience's point of view
- the right tone of voice

and plan to earn a hearing not expect one.

The beginning

This must respect the audience and make it clear that you will be accurately directing your message at them and their needs.
Here you must:

- get off to a good start
- gain attention
- begin to build rapport
- make the group want to listen by starting to satisfy expectations, yet ensure they keep an open mind for what is to come
- position the speaker appropriately (e.g. as confident, expert, credible)
- state your theme, outline how you will go through it (structure) and make it clear this will suit the group (you may also feel it is appropriate to say how long you will take – if the timetable does not – and then stick to that time)

The middle

This is the longest section; it must:

- maintain and develop interest

- develop the case through a logical sequence of sub-themes and points

- illustrate as necessary, with descriptive language and visual aids

- overcome doubts and skepticisms, anticipate specific objections and deal with them and ensure that the building message is seen as of value to those listening

The end

There is a need to finish on a high note, maybe with a flourish. The concluding part of the presentation must:

- summarise and pull together the arguments

- stress benefits to the group

- make clear what action is now appropriate (and often actually ask for a commitment)

- finish on a memorable note

Throughout the presentation the **language** and **gestures** (how you appear and the animation with which you go about the task is just important as how you sound) used must be;

- clear

- natural

- positive

- courteous

and put the emphasis on the key points so that the overall impression is of out-and-out professionalism - your goal is to get your professional approach prompting people to think: 'This is the sort of person I could do business with' (or learn from).

Participipitative techniques

Presentation must be blended with participation to make any training session truly successful. Quite simply involvement makes it more likely that learning will take place and that practice will change as a result; as long ago as Aristotle – who said 'What we have to learn to do, we learn by doing' – this principle was understood.

This principle is now backed up by research and this shows clearly that learning is more likely if participation is involved, and that retention of what is put over is much more likely. Because of this the more you can create involvement in the session – especially if this takes the form of actually practising new techniques, the more likely it is that learning will be carried over and change real work practises for the better.

Prompting involvement can utilise a number of techniques, some as simple as asking a question, others more complex to set up, such as role-playing which is very much part of the proceedings here and about which more guidance follows. Here we review some of the ways to get people involved.

Role-playing is not always well conducted. It is important to address any concerns the group may have about it, perhaps based on prior, and poor, experience. Stressing the positive benefits, making it clear they will be well briefed and that it is an opportunity will help get over any misapprehensions. The key benefits should be seen as useful.

The process starts as soon as the session begins.

A number of factors within the overall introductions and initial formalities can be used to break the ice and begin to get people involved. It is often important for people to realise early on that they will not be able simply to sit and listen, they will be expected to contribute. Such initial initiatives include:

- issuing a simple instruction: 'May I ask you just to fill in the name card in front of you before we continue'

- asking for individual to speak, perhaps to each other (where they do not all know each other): 'Introduce yourself to your immediate neighbour', for example, or: 'Ask the person next to you what they think is the most important objective today'

- using discussion of the brief for the course to get people talking: 'Now I have run through the objectives, can you think of anything else'

- the use of a formal 'ice-breaker' exercise (as set out at the beginning of the workshop material.

Once the session is under way, and exercises and role-plays apart, much of the participation hangs round the use of questions – both fielding those asked and using questions to prompt discussion and comment. To avoid questions interfering with the smooth flow of the session, yet utilise them to best effect needs some care; the techniques are different for each kind of question usage. Each is taken in turn.

FIELDING QUESTIONS ASKED

Prompting questions

Some presentations may have a fairly open brief, and questions are very much for the audience to originate. Others may have a more specific brief and questions are needed to help achieve objectives. For example, if someone is presenting a plan to the Board, they may want to see certain points raised, discussed, and know that what they have said at a more formal stage has been clearly understood.

In such circumstances questions may well need to be prompted. The following sets out sufficient information for such purposes, though the principles involved can be utilised in simpler situations.

Put questions precisely

Questions must be put *precisely*. There is an apocryphal story of the question which asks people 'Are you in favour of smoking whilst praying?'; this does not sound very good, and most people will say 'No'. Ask 'Are you in favour of praying whilst smoking?', however, and most will say 'Yes' (is there a time when one should not pray?). Yet both phrases concern the simultaneous carrying out of the two actions. The moral is to be careful to ask the question in the right way, or you may not obtain the answer you want.

Use open questions

Many questions are best phrased as open questions. Thesse cannot be answered yes or no, and so are more likely to prompt discussion. They typically start what, why, where, who, how or can be neatly led into by asking people to:

describe...	explain...	discuss...
justify...	clarify...	illustrate...
outline...	verify...	define...
review...	compare...	critique...

Directing questions

The first decision is when to take questions. This can be seen as a compromise because:

- questions allowed at any time can disrupt the planned balance of presentation, unless you exercise control
- delaying questions to the very end can frustrate the group and give you a false sense of security that the earlier points have been accepted
- discouraging questions or leaving no time for them is poor training.

You may therefore plan to take questions after each main point. Whatever you do, tell the group the rules; allow time in the presentation for the chosen methodology to work.

As you handle questions *from* the group you may find it useful to use the following techniques:

- Acknowledge the question and questioner.
- Ensure, as necessary, that the question is heard and understood by the rest of the group.
- If in doubt as to what is meant probe to clarify, and restate it back if necessary.
- Give short informative answers whenever possible. Link to other parts of your message, as appropriate.

If you opt, which you may want to, for questions at any time, remember it is perfectly acceptable to:

- Hold them for a moment until you finish making a point
- Delay them, saying you will come back to it, in context in, say, the next session. (Then you must remember. Make a note of both the point and who made it.)
- Refuse them. Some may be irrelevent or likely to lead to too much of a digression, but be *careful* not to do this too often, to respect the questioner's feelings, and to explain why you are doing so
- If you don't know the answer, you *must* say so. You can offer to find out, you can see if anyone else in the group knows, you can make a note of it for later, but if you attempt, unsuccessfully, to answer you lose credibility. No one, in fact, expects you to be ominiscient, so do not worry about it: if you are well prepared it will not happen often in any case.

Asking questions

The questions you ask can check understanding or prompt discussion and make the group think round a point, building their understanding. They will retain information better if there is an element of finding out involved in its aquisition rather than only 'being told'.

There are several ways of directing questions; they can be:

- **overhead questions**, put to the group generally, and useful for opening up a subject (if there is no response, then you can move on to the next method):

    'Right, what do you think the key issue here is? Anyone?'

- **overhead and then directed at an individual**, useful to make the whole group think before looking for an answer from one person:

    'Right, what to you think the key issues here are? Anyone? ... John, what do you think?'

- **direct to individual**, useful for obtaining individual responses, testing for understanding:

    'John, what do you think ... ?'

- **non-reponse rhetorical**, useful where you want to make a point to one or more persons in the group without concentrating on anyone in particular, or for raising a question you would expect to be in the group's mind and then answering it yourself:

    'What's the key issue? Well, perhaps it's ...'

All these methods represent very controlled discussion, i.e. leader ... team member ... leader ... another team member (or more), but ... back to the leader. Two other types help to open up a discussion:

- **re-directed questions**, useful to make others in the group answer any individual's answer.

    'That's a good point John. What do you think the answer is, Mary?'

- **developmental questioning**, where you take the answer to a previous question and move it around the audience, building on it:

  'Having established that, how about …?'

Whichever of the above is being used, certain principles should be borne in mind. For questioning to be effective, the following general method may be a useful guide to the kind of sequence that can be employed:

- **State the question clearly and concisely**. Questions should relate directly to the subject being discussed. Whenever possible they should require people to think, to draw on their past experiences, and relate them to the present circumstances.

- **Ask the question first to the group rather than to an individual**. If the question is directed to a single individual, others are off the hook and do not have to think about the answer. Direct, individual questions are more useful to break a general silence in the group, or to involve someone who is not actively participating in the discussion.

- **After asking the question, pause**. Allow a few moments for the group to consider what the answer should be. Then …

- **Ask a specific individual to answer**. The four-step process starts the entire group thinking because they never know who will be called on. Thus everyone has to consider each question you ask, and be ready to participate. Even those who are not called on are still involved.

To be sure of using an effective questioning technique, there are some points which should be **avoided**, such as:

- **Asking yes or no questions**. Participants can attempt to guess the answer (and may be right). These questions should not be used if you want participants to use their reasoning power and actively participate in the training.

- **Asking tricky questions**. Remember, your purpose is to train people, not to antagonise them or make them look bad. Difficult questions, yes. Tricky, no. Keep personalities and sarcasm out of your questions.

- **Asking unanswerable questions.** You want to provide knowledge, not confusion. Be sure that the knowledge and experience of your group are such that at least some participants can answer the questions you're asking. Never attempt to highlight ignorance by asking questions which the group can't handle.

And this is particularly true when you're trying to draw out a silent trainee and involve him. Be sure he can answer before you ask them the questions.

- **Asking leading questions.** By leading questions, we mean ones in which the trainer indicates the preferred answer in advance: 'Mary, don't you agree that this new form will help solve the problem?' Such questions require little effort on the part of the participant, and little learning takes place. In addition, even if Mary didn't agree, she would probably be uncomfortable saying so. After all, that does not seem to be the answer you want.

- Asking personal questions. Personal questions are usually rather sensitive, even in one-to-one sessions. They are often inappropriate in a group session.

- **Repeating questions.** Don't make a practice of repeating the question for an inattentive person. Doing so simply encourages further inattention and wastes valuable time. Instead, ask someone else to respond. People will quickly learn that they have to listen.

- **Allowing group answers.** Unless writen down, (and then referred to around the group), questions that allow several members of the group to answer are not useful. First, everyone cannot talk at once. Second, with group answers a very few participants may well tend to dominate the session. And third, group answers allow the silent person to hide and not participate as they should.

Note: the one unbreakable rule all training sessions should have, clearly understood and adhered to, is ONLY ONE PERSON MAY TALK AT ONCE (and the leader must be the acknowledged referee and decide who has the floor at any particular moment).

Above all, let your questioning be natural. Ask because you want to know – because you want this information to be shared with the group. Never think of yourself as a quiz master with certain questions that must be asked whether or not they're timely. Let your manner convey your interest in the reponse you're going to get, and be sure that your interest is genuine. Forced, artifical enthusiasm will never fool a group.

No matter how effective your questioning technique may become, never consider yourself so clever that you can manipulate the participants. Manipulation is not its purpose. Instead, questioning should be used to promote and build genuine participation, not in bending the group to your will.

Finally, for questioning to be effective instructional technique you must create the proper atmosphere in which it can flourish. For example, participants should never fear to give an incorrect answer. If wrong answers are discouraged, participants will respond more cautiously. People should never have the feeling that they are asking stupid questions. It cannot be over-emphasized that they should be encourged to ask questions, at any time, about anything they do not understand.

Using exercises

Questions can prompt discussion, which is valuable in two ways:

- people like, and learn from, participation as a process;
- the discussion may well be creative, casting new light on some aspect of the subject;

but, people will learn still more from actually working as a task.

Exercises can be as short as a few minutes or as long as many hours. For the purposes of the present discussion, which relates primarily to short training sessions of perhaps three hours to three days, exercises can be conducted in several ways:

- **individually**: there is a place for participants individually working through an exercise: one benefit is that of letting people work at their own pace, and on their own situations or problems. Protracted individual exercises in a group situation *seem* to be inappropriate, and are therefore best kept short.

- **in pairs**: working in pairs gives some of the advantages of individual exercises, yet involves active participation. It is affected by room layout, and works best when people are seated so that they can simply turn to their neighbours and go straight into an exercise without moving. (Additionally, an individual exercise can then be commented on, or developed in pairs).

- **in syndicates**: working in syndicates takes somewhat longer, and may involve some moving about, but it is useful. There should not be too many in a group, 5–8 perhaps, and you can make it work best by sugesting that:

- a chairperson is promptly elected (or nominated) to control discussion and keep an eye on the time

- a secretary is chosen to keep notes of points agreed

- a presenter is chosen to report back to the main group.

If each exercise has a different chairperson or presenter, everyone is given an active role as syndicate sessions progress, and tasks are spread round the group.

The ultimate form of exercise, particularly for training in interactive skills (and certainly here as we consider selling) is role-playing. This needs careful setting up, and is worth considering in more detail; this is done in the next section.

Role-playing

Any training that attempts to develop an essentially interactive skill must make a firm link between theory and practice. This is perhaps particularly true of selling; its dynamic nature and the need to adapt, deploying techniques as appropriate to each situation, are key lessons to put over. Role-playing is a well-proven way to exemplify the material presented and reviewed and, however participative the proceedings have been in other ways, it is well worth allowing time for such a session.

Role-playing is a powerful technique, though it is not necessarily the easiest activity to organise if you are to obtain the best results from it. It needs preparation, thought and care and ideally draws on the field experience of the trainer (many would see it as difficult to train others in selling unless the leader has some personal experience of actually making sales calls). That said, its value can be considerable and it provides a safe opportunity to practice with no fear of upsetting any real customers, or losing business as a result. As such it may also be regarded as providing an opportunity to experiment in a way that might be regarded as risky in the real world.

Specifically, it provides:

- an opportunity for each individual to obtain feedback on their own performance (not least their own perception of performance)
- examples of common occurences (problems, opportunities or whatever) for further group discussion
- a prompt to participants to think about and thus better understand the buyer's situation as usually some or all of them will take turns in acting out the buyer's role.

Most usually role-playing will use video recording equipment to facilitate playback and discussion of each enacted situation. This is certainly best, and the following section is based largely on this premise, though there is no reason why you cannot handle things more simply. It can work with audio recording only, or just carried out live and followed by review and discussion – though the latter necessitates careful note taking, and keeping the sessions reasonably short, if there is to be accurate recall of exactly what was said.

Before getting into more detail, it is worth considering the simplest form of role-playing which is fundamentally just an informal enactment of a real life situation. For example, if you pose a question that leads into conversation: 'Imagine the buyer says......' and you quote an example of what he might say, then you can ask: 'How would you reply?'. If this last question is directed at a chosen individual participant, with an injunction for him to reply *verbatim*, then it will create a moment of conversation – this can be between yourself and one of the participants, or between two participants. Such a conversation can be continued for just a moment, or for a few minutes, after which the session returns to its normal format. This is role-playing; people are made to think about the topic, not in academic terms, but very much in its day-to-day application Yet there is no formality, none of the equipment, recording and playback more normally associated with role-playing.

At the other end of the scale there is considerable formality, with all the panoply of equipment and recording which can be daunting. I have been involved in role-playing which returns in four main sessions during the day to the same developing scenario, which even uses people from outside the course and the organisation (this, for example, in training in recruitment interviewing skills, where real interviews with actual candidates have been filmed – with the permission or the candidates – to assist in developing key skills); so elaborate forms are certainly possible, and can work well.

To return to the more routine, and start with the dangers, role-playing can fail and, if it does, the cause probably lies among the following:

- over-awareness of the camera
- over-acting to the camera
- a belief that role-playing means acting
- the difficulty of 'performing' in front of one's peers

- poor role-play briefs
- weak management of the role-play
- incomplete or unconstructive feedback after the role-play
- those not role-playing being given nothing to do.

More positively, all role-plays should be organized to achieve one or more of the following objectives:

- reproduce real life as closely as possible
- provide an opportunity to practice difficult situations
- provide an opportunity to practise new skills
- develop confidence
- enhance learning by building on success
- experiment with new approaches
- change negative habits/reinforce positive habits
- fix knowledge and an attitude of professionalism
- promote anaytical skill through self-appraisal and observing others.

The following details four different forms of role-playing which, although these can be adapted, amended and used in a variety of different ways, make useful examples, and show how to make role-playing work well and generate constructive feedback. Though I have described them in terms of video use, there is no reason why they should not be effective without this facility.

The 'classic' role-play. This is where two participants act out a situation to reinforce their sales skill. Assuming a clear objective, and the use of standard video equipment (i.e. camera/tripod, microphone, video recorder and TV monitor), the physical arrangements must be able to comfortably facilitate what needs to take place. The following examples show how this can be achieved. Though, of course, no one sequence of events should be followed slavishly, the following illustrates a typical approach:

- Issue the role-play briefs to the two participants, and allow them time to plan their approachcs. If either is playing himself this should be made clear. It is certainly less confusing if participants use their own names, whatever their roles.

- State the objective, and summarize the briefs for the observers.

- Issue any observation and feedback forms to the observers. (A specific sales training example appears in Figure 1.) Emphasize that theirs is an active role in the learning process.

- Introduce the camera operator (if one is used). Brief him on what he should capture on film, i.e. one participant's role, the other's reactions, or both.

- Indicate when you want the role-play to end, i.e. after a certain time, or when a particular point in the content has been reached.

- Invite questions, ensuring that everyone knows what to do.

- Emphasise that a role-play is a group learning exercise, not an opportunity to test one individual.

- Invite the two role-players to take their places. (Layout needs some thought; examples appear in Figure 2.)

- Take your seat near the video deck, and be prepared to note down the tape numbers of where key points occur during the exchanges

- When the role-play has finished:
  - thank the two participants and invite them to rejoin the group
  - ask the observers to complete their feedback notes
  - ask the two particpants to write down their own impressions of their role-play
  - allow the lead player to comment first, drawing in the other as appropriate
  - ask the observers to offer their initial impressions
  - offer your own initial impressions
  - play back the opening moments of the role-play, using this as your

Figure 1 Observation and feedback form

Participants: Salesman _____ Customer _____

Role play objective: _____

	A+	A	B+	B
How well did the salesman listen to the customer?	[ ]	[ ]	[ ]	[ ]
How well did the salesman's replies satisfy the customer?	[ ]	[ ]	[ ]	[ ]
How clear and understandable were the salesman's questions?	[ ]	[ ]	[ ]	[ ]
How well did the salesman control the interview?	[ ]	[ ]	[ ]	[ ]
What was the salesman's level of product knowledge?	[ ]	[ ]	[ ]	[ ]
What was the salesman's level of competitor product knowledge?	[ ]	[ ]	[ ]	[ ]
How well did the salesman use his sales aids?	[ ]	[ ]	[ ]	[ ]
How well did the salesman spot and use opportunities to conclude the interview positively?	[ ]	[ ]	[ ]	[ ]

General impressions: _____

Recommendations: _____

cue to lead a discussion on particular details
- ensure that the observers' feedback is constructive, and the participants are allowed to respond
- use the video to highlight key points
- at an appropriate point, draw the discussions to a close. Ask for final comments from the observers; invite final comments from the participants and then summarise.

Your summary should be divided into distinct elements: thank and praise the participants; thank the observers; summarize the key learning points which first, directly affect the individual(s), and second, may apply to the group.

• Re-wind the tape and prepare for the next role-play.

The 'carousel' role-play. This role-play involves the situation being started by two participants and, at an appropriate point, being handed over to two others, who continue to act out the same scenario. It is thus a good way of involving more people in the group, more quickly.

Again a typical but not definitive sequence of events illustrates what is involved:

• Divide the complete process into suitable parts (e.g. a sales interview might be divided into the opening, establishing needs, presenting the product/service, handling objections, and gaining a commitment). Ensure that the group understands the basis for the split.

• Divide the group into pairs, and nominate who in each pair will play which role. However, do *not* indicate the phase which each pair will role-play, not least so that everyone will concentrate throughout the proceedings.

• Distribute the Carousel Role-Play Instructions (see example in Figure 3).

• Distribute any necessary Role-Play Briefs. (*Note*: All members of the group should be given the same two briefs, one for each of the roles.)

Figure 2 Layout organization using only the training room

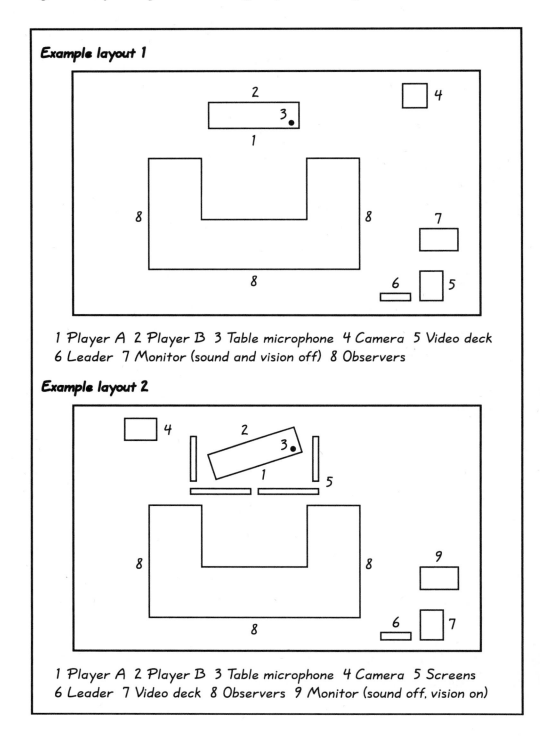

Example layout 1

1 *Player A* 2 *Player B* 3 *Table microphone* 4 *Camera* 5 *Video deck*
6 *Leader* 7 *Monitor (sound and vision off)* 8 *Observers*

Example layout 2

1 *Player A* 2 *Player B* 3 *Table microphone* 4 *Camera* 5 *Screens*
6 *Leader* 7 *Video deck* 8 *Observers* 9 *Monitor (sound off, vision on)*

- Invite or nominate two participants to play the first interview phase.
- Begin the role-play.
- At an appropriate point, stop the role-play and either:
  (i) invite a second pair to continue from that point, or
  (ii) play back and take feedback comments, then invite a second pair to continue.
- When the complete scenario has been role-played, lead a feedback discussion in the same way as for the 'classic' role-play.

The 'silent' role-play. Silent because the scenario is enacted in writing. This is clearly unsuited to anything lengthy, but is very valuable when there is great precision necessary (e.g. the brief moments when a prospecting salesperson introduces his company on the telephone; the succinct description of a key product benefit where the wording must be exactly right).

Again, a typical sequence of events illustrates the process:

- Divide the group into pairs, and brief them about their respective roles. Check that all is clear.
- Then a conversation is acted out and written down – word for word. This is done on the same sheet of paper – passed between the two – so that the developing conversation remains visible in its entirety.
- Once the exchanges are complete the whole conversation can be read out and discussed. (*Note*: This also works well with the leader playing one role and inter-relating with individual members of the group; and also with syndicates discussing, and recording, a measured response.)
- There should be *no* talking between parties during the role-play.
- The real learning will take place during and after the role-play; it teaches the importance of thinking about, clearly expressing and logically structuring what you want to say. Seeing the actual words in black and white can be an object lesson in learning how to focus and clarify spoken presentations.

Figure 3 Carousel role-playing instructions

Objectives
To reinforce skill at _____
To actively involve everyone

1. One of our typical interviews has been broken down into its key phases:

   (i) _____ (iii) _____
   (ii) _____ (iv) _____

2. Each pair will role-play one of these phases.
3. You all have a copy of the same two briefs, one for each role.
4. The first pair will role-play the first interview phase. At an appropriate point their role-play will be stopped and a second pair will be invited to continue the interview without losing its direction and building upon what has already been established. This pair will role-play the second interview phase.
5. Again, at an appropriate point this role-play will be stopped and a third pair will be invited to continue the same interview, also without losing direction and building upon the facts and agreements already established. Their task is to role-play the third interview phase.
6. You must remain alert, listening and taking notes so that whenever it is your turn to take over you are able to maintain the interview momentum.
7. Throughout the interview you may introduce new information. However, if you do, this must:
   - not be designed to 'catch out' the other 'player'
   - not directly contradict whatever has already been established and agreed
   - sensibly reflect real life situations
8. The role plays will continue until a clear conclusion has been reached.
9. The leader may temporarily halt the role-play between pairs either to play back the video recording or to summarize key agreements between the two parties.

The 'triad' role-play. As the name suggests, this involves three people participating in three roles during the role-play session (e.g. a salesperson, a technical support specialist and the buyer; or a salesperson and two involved in the buying decision).

This can either work very like the 'classic' role-play, or the third person can be an observer (but staying 'in character'); thus, the role-play observer's task is to observe, then comment upon the two role-play participants. (Essentially, he plays the leader's role for the moment.)

The remainder of the group have a dual task: to comment on the role-play participants; and to watch and comment on how the observer conducts his feedback.

In the next role-play, the observer moves into participant 'A's' seat, and A moves to the other side of the table and becomes 'B'. 'B' rejoins the group, and a new player takes over as observer (i.e. an element or carousel).

The leader's role is to orchestrate the action and learning, not forgetting that the emphases in this type of role-playing are: the participants and the skills displayed, and the observer and his analysis and appraisal skills.

From the least formal format, mentioned earlier, to the more complex, role-playing is an important tool of sales training. It should not, however, be underestimated in terms of the care and preparation it necessitates. If it moves off track, if it goes badly, then people are made to look inadequate which, understandably, they do not like. Providing participants are clear as to the brief, and understand the purpose of the exercise, and providing that the leader sets up the situation carefully and makes it a risk-free experience, it can add to a training session to meaningful extent. Its greatest contribution is not in providing a test of individuals, but in creating discussion of examples and situations which the whole group can use, and from which approaches for the future can be constructed.

Finally in this section, there should be a recognition that not all the people in the group are the same. Everyone is an individual, everyone responds to the group situation differently; but you have to work with them all.

The use of training films

However stimulating the training, however much the participants are involved, participants may still be stimulated even more by greater variety of training methodology. And a classic way of providing variety in recent years has been the training film. There is a profusion of material available and good ones can do much more than provide variety.

Sales techniques are well covered so such films are worth a comment here. First the dangers: some films are promoted as being, or seem to be, self-contained; that is their topic can be put over solely by showing the film. This may be true of certain basic issues, but films will nearly always have a more pronounced effect if they are used as an integral part of a longer session.

How do they help training to be more effective? In several ways:

- first, film provides a different set of memories; through visualisation, character, humour or whatever they put a different complexion on the message and are a clear aid to retention

- they vary the pace

- they can introduce a topic, particularly to lead into discussion that extends its review

- they can act to summarise at the end of a session

or they can sometimes be used in segments, watching part of a film, pausing for comment or discussion, then returning to the film. However, they are intended to fit in, and whatever role they are intended to have, their effective use is dependent on having a clear objective not only for the course itself, but for the particular session of which the film is part. If you are clear on the point to be made and the result you hope to prompt, then, having considered whether a film will help, the next task is to select a suitable film. Most providers put out catalogues and it may be worth seeking to be listed on their mailing lists to help you keep up to date with exactly what is available.

There are two main types of film:

Right way/wrong way: These may or may not have one continuing story line; either way they tend to start with incidents illustrating how *not* to go about the illustrated task. Then, in the second part of the film they set out examples of effective practice, and also comment on how this is done in clear steps. Often these can be suitable to use in parts.

Case studies. These have a strong story line and the training message emerges from the incidents shown; again there is usually a clear summary or highlighting of key points. Usually these are best used by showing them without pause.

Both kinds, and most film providers, suppliers provide good back up trainers guides in printed form. The best of these are excellent, and how helpful you find particular ones may usefully form part of a decision as to which film to use.

Films come in a variety of styles. Some are humorous, some to the point where there is a danger of humour overwhelming the message; others utilise a background that may or may not be appropriate for you (a large or small company, a technical or non technical product, for instance). The main providers all produce comprehensive catalogues and offer a variety of ways of previewing their films – an unbreakable rule should be never to use any film you have not seen through in its entirety and had time to integrate into the session. From this selection onwards it may make sense to adopt almost a checklist approach to how you use a film – see box.

Using films

- View the chosen film in its entirety
- Make notes regarding:
  - significant scenes, points or dialogue that you may wish to quote or refer to after the film has been shown
  - key training points
  - additional points (sometimes necessitating 'reading between the lines')
  - prompts to discussion, and specific questions you will ask the group
  - names of characters or other details you may want to quote (it hardly positions you as an expert if you appear unfamiliar with the material)
  - any pause points you want to use when the film is shown to the group (during which you will use discussion, role-play or other methods to exemplify the message)
- Read, and if useful annotate, the film 'trainers booklet', (even when you hire films these can usually be retained) which often contain more detail on the topic than appears in the film
- View the film again before using it on the session

Relating these comments back to the workshop described, a film or films (it is unlikely that you would want more than two within the content and extent of the material described) may well be useful to such a session. But it is by no means essential, and if film is used time must be taken for it to slot into the session and also, earlier, for its use to be prepared. The choice is yours. One final point: never use a film which does not really suit the session you aim to conduct, it will end up not simply failing to add to the proceedings but actually being a distraction.

Afterword

So, at the end of the workshop, or at the end of the material, having checked through preparatory to conducting the work shop, what next? It is important to end by putting certain matters in context.

First, selling is a complex social skill. This workshop is designed to allow you to cover all the fundamental techniques that are the basis of being successful in selling. Beyond that success is dependent on practice. Such practice must do two things:

- It must deploy the techniques appropriately, customer by customer, day by day, meeting by meeting so as to maximise the chances of success in the short term.

- It must take place with a certain awareness of how it is being done, and how well it is all working, both to fine tune its precise application in an individual meeting to ensure the best chance of success.

Second, it must be accepted that the nature of selling is dynamic, the inescapable fact is that what works best will change over time. All sorts of pressures, competition, customer attitudes and so on change over time and affect how selling works. The best salespeople recognise this and work actively to keep themselves up to date. No one ever learns an infallible way to sell and can then simply apply it slavishly. Long term it can be the lack of this on-going fine-tuning of method that separates even the good salesperson from the best, with the less aware lagging behind.

Thus, at the end of the day, it is right for you to refer to what has been covered as fundamental techniques. There is an old saying that a person can either have, say, five year's experience or one year's experience multiplied by five. In selling, not only is the former the only way to ensure techniques are kept up to the mark, it is also surely what the people will want for themselves. Motivation, so important to the sales process, is surely not enhanced by believing that the job is essentially repetitive.

All this leads to the same conclusion. If you are looking for a note on which to end that links what has been done to the future, then perhaps the most valuable thoughts that you can leave with people are these:

- selling is, must be, dynamic
- performance can be maintained and improved in light of this by conscious practice
- the workshop provides the foundation (and should provide some immediate ideas and assistance) beyond that the only coach that is there to assist all the time is the individual himself
- the best salespeople recognise this, act accordingly, and achieve better results – and greater job satisfaction – as a result.

The future

Not only is selling a dynamic process, as has been said, it is also likely to increase in complexity in the future along with the way in which markets themselves develop. On the one hand there are always new – sometimes almost magical – approaches being promoted to assist the average salesperson to become a star performer. Many of these are cosmetic or simply not credible. On the other hand the fundamental principles of selling – identifying needs, talking benefits, proving the claims that are made about the product or service – are likely to remain important.

Beyond both there are other skills involved and other factors that dictate their relevance that are important for the future. A number of such are listed below, and may be worth keeping in mind or mentioning, particularly at the end of the training session to conclude with a look ahead:

- **the commercial environment**: selling is a front line activity and is bound to be subject to the prevailing economic and commercial pressures of the moment. Whether the market is in recession or a competitor has just launched a new product that makes selling yours more difficult, the sales approach has to include an appropriate response. There tends always to be something of this sort to actively consider and build into the way sales-people work

- **the marketing strategy**: selling does not exist in a corporate vacuum, it is part of the marketing and promotional mix. It must work in a way that is both effective and fits with the overall strategy of the organisation. For example, if the promotional platform stresses technical or service excellence then everything the salespeople do with customers must reflect that image. This too is a dynamic area and activity must always reflect current strategic issues

- **the buyers' attitude and expectations**: whoever the buyer is (and it may be more than one person) selling only works if it fits with their thinking and the way in which purchase decisions are really made. Sales activity must always observe and reflect this in a practical way

- **additional skills**: for all the reasons that have now been given about the changing nature of the sales process, it is likely that, in addition to the foundations skills, there will be additional factors that are important at different times or to different types of selling. Long-term, these will need addressing also in terms of skills development; such may include:

Major account management: large accounts are different in nature as well as scale. They demand more analysis, different handling at every stage and must be planned, managed and developed in a way that ensures current targets are met and which holds and builds for the future.

Formal Presentation: many sales situations, not least with the major customers referred to above, need not just effective handling one to one across the desk, they need group communication as well. For instance, a buying committee may be involved and want a presentation formally made to them by several competing potential suppliers. The successful salesperson who is involved in this kind of situation must be at least as good on his feet as in a more intimate meeting; and this demands additional skills.

Negotiation: this has been referred to previously; it is a separate yet overlapping set of skills to selling, and these, too, may be an essential part of some kinds of selling, often necessitating a high level of financial numeracy also.

Documentation: another skill essential to some forms of sale is to be persuasive in writing. Proposals, reports and other documents are often not of the same standard as face to face selling in an organisation. Somehow the skill of persuasive writing is not seen as one of the stocks in trade in the same way as other skills (or, commonly, it is simply in a rut with documents being reiterated in a manner based on a previous style long needing a rethink). This too may present an opportunity for those who get it right, in a situation where prevailing standards are perhaps felt by buyers to leave something to be desired.

These, and doubtless other points which could be made, are both illustrative of the key issues and representative of the way in which the selling job is going. I remember once telephoning a salesman who had been to see me and being told by his company's switchboard that he was out, coupled with the observation that: 'He's not often in the office, he's only a salesman'. Only? Anyone in selling can do with a great deal more support than that; but the problem remains. It is all too easy for people to be seen as 'only a salesman', indeed, it can be possible that they begin to believe it themselves. Sales training should address issues that are based on the opposite view, that selling is a vital and complex task that can only be successfully done if it is professional. Salespeople that really believe not only that they are professional, but that it matters, will tend to produce better results than any that doubt it or see the whole process as merely routine.

If your training session builds motivation in this respect and acts to create a culture of professionalism as well as the knowledge and skill to do the job, it will be well worth the time it takes; if this publication helps you do both it will also prove worth while.

Postscript

This material is designed to be, and is I hope, self-sufficient. Selling is, as has been firmly said, a dynamic process. While in part it is common sense, there are not only a number of approaches and techniques involved, but their ultimate success is dependent on the orchestration of the whole process. Training, too, can be a complex process. Many involved in either will readily admit they continue to learn throughout their career, so despite the self-sufficient intention of this book it is appropriate to mention the need to check other references.

If you have found the way things are presented here useful, then two from the same author may be useful:

The Selling Edge (a Piatkus paperback) sets out a review of the sales job, and particularly which areas of the techniques involved most strongly increase the likelihood of a good success rate. As the **Background notes** here are drawn, in part, from this, it may make a useful follow up handout.

Running an Effective Training Session (Gower) is the practical guide I wish I had been given when I started in training, and it sets out effective approach-es for trainer and line manager alike. I am grateful to the pub-lishers for permission to drawn on certain aspects of this book in Section 3 of this volume.

Both fit well with this volume. This may be a biased recommendation, but if a manual on selling cannot contain one unashamed plug, what can?

P. F.

READY MADE ACTIVITIES RESOURCE PACKS

Developing your Staff
Selling Skills
Customer Care Skills
Negotiation Skills
Presentation Skills
Financial Skills

In a high pressure environment you need to bring your team up to speed quickly and effectively. Waiting for the right course can waste time.

The *Ready Made Activities Resource Packs* give you access to material to develop your own skills and those of your staff in vital areas such as finance, negotiation and customer care.

You can see how simple it is to improve the skills of your staff and save your company thousands of pounds by completing the training yourself. It couldn't be easier with our unique new *Ready Made Activities Resource Pack* – and you don't have to be an expert or even have any training experience to use them!.

These special versions of the Ready Made Activities series come with the full endorsement of the Institute of Management and are available in a Ringbound Presentation Folder containing all the information you could need to present the new skills to your team.

All the *Ready Made Activities Resource Packs* come complete with
- Overhead Transparencies – impress your colleagues and your bosses with a professional presentation
- Free Video – reinforce the message or open your sessions with this ice-breaker
- Photocopiable Handouts – give your staff the key points of your presentation to take away and refer to again and again.

All this and more for only £120.00*

Available direct from Pitman Publishing
Telephone 071 379 7383 or fax 071 240 5771

*Price correct at time of going to press but is subject to change without notice

ORDER FORM

Simply complete and return to:
Professional Marketing Department, Pitman Publishing, 128 Long Acre,
London, WC2E 9AN, UK
Telephone 071 379 7383 or fax on 071 240 5771

Quantity   *Total*

_____   **Developing your Staff Resource Pack** @ £120.00   _____

_____   **Selling Skills Resource Pack** @ £120.00   _____

_____   **Customer Care Skills Resource Pack** @ £120.00   _____

_____   **Negotiation Skills Resource Pack** @ £120.00   _____

_____   **Presentation Skills Resource Pack** @ £120.00   _____

_____   **Financial Skills Resource Pack** @ £120.00   _____

☐ I would like to join the free information service

Postage and packing please add:

UK   add £3.00 per order
Elsewhere in Europe   add £5.00 for the first pack, £3.00 per pack thereafter
Rest of World   add £9.00 for the first pack, £6.00 per pack thereafter

Payment (Please complete)

☐ Please charge my Access/Visa/Mastercard/ Barclaycard/Diners Club/American
   Express for £ _____ (total)

Card Number ☐☐☐☐☐☐☐☐☐☐☐☐☐☐☐☐   Expiry Date _____

Indicate both card billing and delivery address if these differ.

☐ Please invoice me at the address below for £ _____ (total)

☐ I enclose a cheque payable to Pitman Publishing for £ _____ (total)

Name _____   Position _____

Company _____

Address _____

_____   Postcode _____

Telephone number (in case of order query) _____

EC Customers please supply your VAT number _____